Jobs and the Rhineland Model

Ian Davidson

FEDERAL TRUST REPORT

THE FEDERAL TRUST

The Federal Trust works through research and education towards the widening and deepening of the European Union as well as to enhance the European policy of the United Kingdom

The Trust conducts enquiries, promotes seminars and conferences and publishes reports and teaching materials on the European dimension.

Its current and future work programme includes studies of long-term change in Europe, civic education in Europe, and the future of the European Parliament. Up-to-date information about the Federal Trust can be found on the internet at www.fedtrust.co.uk.

The Trust is the UK member of TEPSA (the Trans-European Policy Studies Association).

The Federal Trust is a registered charity and expresses no political view of its own.

The Trust's latest publication is Andrew Duff (ed.), *The Treaty of Amsterdam: Text and Commentary*, 1997.

The front cover features the Kronprinzen Bridge in Berlin. The bridge across the River Spree was first built in 1879, and has been rebuilt since the fall of the Berlin Wall, spanning the old divide between East and West. The EU contributed DM 11 m towards the total cost of DM 35 m. In the background is the Reichstag, currently being rebuilt to the design of a British architect.

Published by the Federal Trust
Dean Bradley House
52 Horseferry Road
London SW1P 2AF

ISBN 0 90157 364 7
The Federal Trust is a Registered Charity
Marketing and Distribution by Sweet & Maxwell Ltd
Printed in the European Union

Contents

Acknowledgments

The Federal Trust set up a group to study the problems of work and welfare in Europe in February 1997.

I am indebted to all members of the study group for their commitment and expertise, and especially to Dick Taverne, its chairman, to Ian Davidson, its rapporteur, and to Harry Cowie, who acted as its secretary. Richard Blackman was our valuable research officer.

Members of the study group served in their personal capacities. They do not necessarily concur with all the views expressed in the Report, but they support its general conclusions and welcome its publication. The membership was:

Bill Callaghan	Trades Union Congress
Harry Cowie	Federal Trust
Ian Davidson	Financial Times
Ronald Dore	London School of Economics
Andrew Duff	Federal Trust
Michael Emerson	London School of Economics
David Goodhart	Prospect
Charles Handy	Author and broadcaster
Lutz Hoffmann	German Institute for Economic Research
Christopher Huhne	IBCA Sovereign Ratings
Dominic Johnson	Confederation of British Industry
John Kay	Said Business School, Oxford
John Morley	European Commission
Bettina Nürk	Deutsche Bank Research
John Pinder	Federal Trust
Keith Richardson	European Round Table of Industrialists
David Soskice	Social Science Research Centre, Berlin
Lord Taverne	Prima Europe
Harald Trabold	German Institute for Economic Research
Stefanie Wahl	Institute for Economy and Society, Bonn

The Federal Trust is grateful to the European Commission, the Anglo-German Foundation for the Study of Industrial Society and the London Office of the European Parliament for their support.

The study group was grateful to have taken evidence from the following:

Ronald Cohen	Apax Partners; EASDAQ
Alberto Giovanni	Long-Term Capital Management
Stephen Nickell	University of Oxford
Vincent Palmade	McKinsey, Paris
Vincent Pelade	French Embassy, London
Peter Robinson	London School of Economics
Denis Snower	Birkbeck College
Rinze Tjeerdsma	Confederation of Netherlands Industry

The Federal Trust welcomes comments on its Reports. They should be addressed to me at the Federal Trust, Dean Bradley House, 52 Horseferry Road, London SW1P 2AF.

Andrew Duff

Director

December 1997

Foreword

Unemployment is perhaps the biggest problem facing the European Union. The question which our study group examined was whether its persistence in so many EU countries was due to a fundamental defect in the European social model.

The Anglo-Saxon view, which seems to be embraced by the present Labour government in Britain as well as its Conservative predecessor, is that the key to lower unemployment lies in greater labour market flexibility and deregulation. Frequently the recent record of the United States and Britain is contrasted favourably with that of Germany, France, Spain and other continental countries. The success of the former in reducing unemployment, it is argued, has been due to an open market approach, relatively low taxation and flexible labour markets. The lack of success of the latter is blamed on high taxes, excessive social security provision and labour market rigidities.

We concentrated specifically on the so-called Rhineland model most closely associated with the German economy, not only because Germany is the largest economy in Europe, but because it was until recently the most successful and now seems to find unemployment an almost intractable problem. We started by asking whether such a model could in fact be identified and, if so, what its basic characteristics were, and then sought to probe beneath the rather facile generalisations which have sometimes dominated the debate between the Anglo-Saxons and the social capitalists.

Few of the generalisations survived our scrutiny. Like some of the reports from the OECD and the European Commission, we did find that certain kinds of inflexibility and over-regulation, as well as high social security burdens, contribute to the high unemployment in the EU. But macro-economic factors, and in particular the consequences of German unification, have played an even greater part. Further, there are other aspects of the Rhineland model which have, or can have, beneficial employment effects: for example, its association with a high level of skills among the workforce.

The success of the Dutch economy since the early 1980s suggests that there is no reason why the virtues of the Rhineland model and its emphasis on consensus cannot be combined with a greater degree of flexiblility and deregulation and a greater reliance on open capital markets. But in any case it is unlikely that the social values on which most of the continental economies are based will be abandoned. The Rhineland model may have to undergo structural change to create more jobs and make the single currency area a success. But there is no need in our view to throw out the baby with the bathwater. Reports of the coming death of the model will turn out to be greatly exaggerated.

The quality of our deliberations was greatly enhanced by the participation of so many people from so many countries. We are most grateful to all those who took the trouble to travel long distances to play such an invaluable part.

We are particularly grateful to our rapporteur, Ian Davidson, who wove the disparate and sometimes confusing strands of our discussions into what I believe to be a coherent report that should make a useful contribution to a vital topic.

Dick Taverne
Chairman

Jobs and the Rhineland Model: A Federal Trust Report

Summary

1. Free market critics claim that the institutions and social mechanisms of the European economies, which they sometimes characterise collectively as 'the Rhineland Model', are to blame for the fact that European countries have generally been performing less well in recent years than the United States.

2. This judgment is too simplistic. First, there are large differences between European countries, both in their institutions and in their performance. Second, the current contrast, between Europe's serious economic problems and America's triumphant success, is a recent phenomenon. It is not so long since the best performing European countries were doing better than the US.

3. Is there such a thing as the Rhineland Model, to be contrasted to the American Model? Perhaps: but if so, it is essentially a question of social and political values, rather than of specific institutions or detailed mechanisms.

4. At the level of values, many European countries share an emphasis on consensus and negotiation, a high priority for social solidarity, and a large role for the welfare state. But at the level of practical institutions, the national differences between European countries are great: there is no single and universal Rhineland Model.

5. The most powerful immediate forces behind Europe's high level of unemployment have come from the cyclical recession, aggravated by two politico-strategic shocks: German unification, and the run-up to EMU. The initial euphoric boom of German unification was followed by a firm anti-inflation crackdown by the Bundesbank, while Europe's emergence from recession was not made easier by the strict budget-cutting required by EMU.

6. The Rhineland Model, by contrast, has not been a prime mover in the deteriorating employment situation in Europe. But it has obviously played an important contributory role, in the sense that it preserved entrenched protective practices which must be reformed if Europe is to adapt to the rapidly changing circumstances of the world economy. To

that extent, today's unemployment is partly a symptom of wide-spread reluctance to introduce long-delayed reforms.

7. In Germany, however, one important contributory factor behind the steep rise in unemployment was not the Rhineland Model itself, but on the contrary the breakdown of the Rhineland Model. The central assumption of the model is that it is based on negotiation and moderation. But the boom and bust which followed German unification was due in significant degree to the breakdown of the previous moderation in wage settlements.

8. It is clear that European countries cannot avoid far-reaching reforms in their national welfare systems, and radical liberalisation of their markets. Most need to reduce the burdens of social security contributions and other non-wage labour costs which militate against employment. They also need to rein in the overall costs of welfare, whose accumulated costs impose increasingly heavy burdens on national budgets.

9. But since the Rhineland Model depends heavily on consensus and negotiation, it may be naturally slower to adapt to shocks and circumstances of structural change than the classic free-market model. The test of the viability of the Rhineland Model will be the skill and leadership of the politicians in persuading the voters and the social partners of the need for change.

10. Far-reaching reforms, which in many cases will include de-regulation, will certainly be necessary to improve Europe's competitiveness. But not all the institutions and regulations of the Rhineland Model are necessarily bad for employment. And the necessary reforms will not by themselves be sufficient for solving the unemployment crisis, unless there are also effective macro-economic policies for the promotion of economic growth.

11. Many European countries have been slow to introduce the changes required in the new era of global competition: deregulation, privatisation and liberalisation, plus discipline on the budgetary costs of welfare, and restraint in the distribution of welfare benefits. But just as European countries differ widely in their manifestation of the Rhineland Model, so they also differ widely in their record on reform.

12. The UK and the Netherlands have been singled out by the OECD for the success of their reform record, and both have reduced inflation

and unemployment, and achieved faster economic growth. But whereas Britain followed the classic free-market route of deregulation and privatisation, the Netherlands achieved comparable results, not by breaking with the Rhineland Model, but by using its social virtues of consensus and negotiation to maximum advantage.

13. The reform process is proving much more difficult in Germany and France. In France, in particular, de-regulation, privatisation and welfare reform have been bitterly resisted by vested interests and by significant parts of the political class. In fact, it is not yet clear if the new government or the electorate are convinced of the virtues of the free market, or persuaded that fundamental reforms are unavoidable.

14. The characteristic failing of the Rhineland Model may be its tendency to over-regulation, its characteristic virtue the high premium on social solidarity. The characteristic failing of the free-market or US Model may be its tendency to produce growing inequality and social division.

15. The question facing European countries is whether, as a matter of political choice, they can salvage the social virtues of the system, but reform its excesses; or whether free market critics are right to claim that the Rhineland system will be swept away.

16. This question is now becoming all the more urgent with the imminent move to Economic and Monetary Union (EMU). This will restrict monetary and budgetary policy freedom at the national level, and will therefore require greater flexibility and adaptability in the social and labour market domains.

17. Most of the necessary reforms will obviously have to be carried out in the member states by the member states. But since these reforms will be essential for the success of the programme for Economic and Monetary Union and the completion of the Single Market, there will also be a vital role at European Union level for the identification and bench-marking of best practices, for mutual surveillance and the promotion of cross-border mobility.

1. Introduction

Can Europe's economies compete in the brave new world of globalisation and technological change, and at the same time preserve the social and political values which are characteristic of these ancient nation states? That was the subject of our Federal Trust enquiry, and the central question in it was, simply, can Europe resolve its unemployment crisis?

High and persistent structural unemployment is by common consent one of the most serious and widespread economic problems of industrial countries in the 1990s, especially in Europe. Joblessness has been rising steadily in Europe since at least 1990, and the average level of unemployment in the European Union now stands at a historically high figure of over 11 per cent.

This is now such a big problem for many European governments, that it has become one of their central joint pre-occupations. In 1993, the European Commission, under Jacques Delors, published a special White Paper on *Growth, Competitiveness, Employment*, in the hope of galvanising the governments of the European Union to take active new steps to improve Europe's dismal record in job creation. In 1994 the OECD launched its comprehensive Jobs Study, on measures for combating unemployment, which is still under way. And this year the European Union summit at Amsterdam issued a fervent resolution on the importance of keeping employment at the top of Europe's political agenda.

The experience of the United States has been completely different. There, unemployment has been falling steadily since 1992. It now stands at only 5.4 per cent, and it is forecast to go on falling over the next two years.

Some of the immediate factors behind Europe's current economic difficulties are obviously specific and conjunctural. They include the upheaval caused by the fall of the Berlin Wall and the unification of Germany after 1989, the enormous cost of the consequent budgetary flows from West Germany to prop up the East German economy, and the wider deflationary effects of budgetary and monetary tightening across Europe in preparation for the launch of Economic and Monetary Union in the European Union.

But some commentators have drawn a more general conclusion, that the contrast between Europe's economic difficulties and America's apparently effortless economic success, is not just a demonstration of the effectiveness and skilfulness of American economic management, but is a confirmation of the essential structural differences between the socio-economic systems in Europe and America.

The United States, they say, represents an advanced example of a free-enterprise economy: open, deregulated, individualistic, inventive and competitive. By contrast, it is said, the European economies are typically much more collectivist: corporatist, consensual, and interventionist; dominated by trades unions, obsessed with equality, and riddled with welfarism.

The superiority of the American free-enterprise model, according to this argument, is being daily demonstrated by its flexibility and responsiveness to the new challenges of globalisation and rapid structural and technological change, and the bottom line of this superiority is that it is showing up in faster economic growth, more job creation and lower unemployment.

By contrast, the shortcomings of the European or so-called 'Rhineland' model, it is said, are being demonstrated by the extreme social and political difficulties which European countries are going through, as they attempt to adapt to these new challenges. And the bottom line of this inferiority is that it is showing up in slower economic growth, less job creation and higher unemployment.

Some analysts predict that the so-called 'Rhineland model' will be unable to survive in the new global economy, and that Europe's cosy collectivist arrangements, and above all the extravagance of its welfare systems, are bound to be swept away in the new internationally competitive environment.

In our enquiry, we did not hear persuasive evidence which would support such a radical conclusion, though it is clear that Europe needs to engage in far-reaching reforms, including reforms of the Rhineland system, if it is to be able to meet the major challenges of the new world economic environment.

But it was not our purpose to provide categoric let alone simple answers to these difficult dilemmas. Nor do we claim that this report is a definitive or comprehensive survey of the issues at stake. But we hope that the evidence we have surveyed will shed light on the problem from various angles, will show that the dilemmas are more complex than is sometimes suggested, and will in any case contribute to the debate.

2. Is there a Rhineland Model?

Michel Albert, the French businessman and essayist, was one of the first to propound the idea that there are such deep differences between Europe and America, in the way their economies operate, that they can be said to constitute two different models. The American model, he believed, was based on individual success and short-term financial profit; whereas the European system, though equally capitalistic, was based on group success, long-term planning, and the pursuit of consensus.

Albert maintained that the typical European model was to be found in Germany, the Benelux countries, Switzerland and Northern Europe; strikingly, he did not include either France or Italy. So he called it the Rhineland Model.

Albert identified a number of key characteristics of the Rhineland Model: enormously powerful banks, which encompass financial functions carried out in the American model by stock exchanges and money markets; power-sharing and negotiation in the conduct of company management; power-sharing and devolution in the conduct of politics; and a high value on egalitarianism, collective welfare, and the social market.

Some analysts have refined on Michel Albert's concept, by identifying more precisely the institutions and structures of the Rhineland Model. For example, one might list six typical characteristics as follows:

- Businesses are constrained by systems of co-determination to treat employees as stakeholders on a par with shareholders, and to regard the maintenance of employment as an explicit management objective.

- Return on capital is a lower priority than in the US.

- The stock exchange plays a much smaller role in the provision of capital than in the US, and the big banks a much bigger role. Venture capital markets are much less developed.

- There is, by negotiation, a greater uniformity of wage levels, and a higher degree of equality than in the US.

• There is widespread regulation of employment.

• There is consensus support for welfare systems.

• There is heavy expenditure on social security.

Such definitional refinement is valuable for its insights into the working of the system. But such precision is not really necessary for the purposes of our enquiry, for at least three reasons.

1. The essential characteristics of the Rhineland Model are more a set of social and political value systems and attitudes, than the specific institutions and mechanisms by which they are translated into practice, which differ widely between European countries.

2. Albert's paradigm does not include France or Italy; yet for the purposes of today's debate, about the future viability of the Rhineland Model, the similarities between France and Germany are obviously more important than the differences.

3. The forces of globalisation and technological change could bring about, indeed are already bringing about, changes in Europe's economic institutions. For example: the demographic ageing of the European population is likely to have a multiplier effect on economic and financial reforms in Europe. The new constraints of fiscal austerity required by Economic and Monetary Union ensure that ballooning national pension liabilities will have to be met through some forms of private funding. This must lead to a vast transformation of the role of banks, of stock markets and of pension funds in Europe; but it is not obvious why it should lead to an abandonment of the social and political value systems underlying the Rhineland Model.

Free-market critics may believe that the reforms that will be required will represent progressive approximations towards the American model. But the test for Europe will be whether it will be possible to combine free-market reforms with Rhineland-type social and political value systems. Some European analysts argue that if reform efforts in Europe have too often been unsuccessful, it is because there has been too much emphasis on the social and too little on reform.

At the most general level, it seems plausible to suppose that there could be an element of truth in the idea that in many or most European countries the economic systems and institutions are recognisably similar or related, and recognisably distinct from those of other countries; in this case, specifically distinct from those of America. The nations and the states of Western Europe have an immensely long history of mutual interaction and influence, and it is reasonable to suppose that they may share common or overlapping political, social, cultural and economic values. If so, it would be consistent that these common or overlapping values might be manifested in recognisably related social behaviour.

In any case, the most general sense of the Albert proposition is that European economic behaviour is different from American economic behaviour in a number of important ways, all of which essentially revolve around notions of organised negotiation, political consensus and social solidarity: more government intervention and regulation; more public social institutions; more state ownership of industry; more powerful trades unions and other organised economic interest groups; more generous social welfare and health systems; and heavier taxation. Up to a point, this catalogue of characteristics does seem to describe what we can observe, or at least used to be able to observe, in many European countries.

Of course, even if we accept the general validity of the idea, it is clear that the European model is not uniform. Sweden has long appeared the very model of a social-democrat country, but it has never gone in for large-scale state ownership of industry; whereas Italy, which used to appear the very model of a Christian Democrat country, has long had a very large state-owned industry sector. Nor is the European model static. State-owned industries are progressively being privatised in many countries, trades unions are generally less powerful than they used to be, and markets are increasingly deregulated.

Nevertheless, it still seems fair to say that European economic arrangements are more often intended to give higher priority to collective welfare and social solidarity than those in the US; whereas American economic arrangements, by contrast, seem mainly intended to give more prominence to freedom, deregulation, competition, personal responsibility, individual initiative, and private enterprise.

There is some debate whether Britain really belongs in the same 'Rhineland' category as the main continental countries, or whether it belongs more naturally by its economic arrangements in an 'Anglo-Saxon' category together with the US and some Commonwealth countries. Perhaps the truth is that Britain is uneasily suspended in mid-Atlantic, sharing some of the characteristics of continental Europe, and some of the characteristics of the US. Britain's financial and legal institutions for example, resemble those of the US more than those of continental Europe. But its political and social institutions seem to have at least as much in common with those of continental Europe as with those of the US.

The previous British Conservative government used to stress Britain's natural affinities with the US; but this was obviously at least in part the reflection of its political ambivalence towards the European Union. And the new Labour Government has strongly endorsed some of the principles of American-style economic liberalism, conspicuously the idea of labour 'flexibility'.

And yet even if Britain's political leaders do not now believe it should be a paid-up member of the Rhineland Club, it is nevertheless impossible to deny the facts of history, in which Britain shares with Germany and Sweden the paternity of some of the key characteristics of the 'Rhineland Model', including a large welfare state, social solidarity in care for the sick and the aged, and an important and publicly recognised role for the trades unions. And to the extent that some version of moderate 'Socialism' has long been respectable in British politics, as in almost all other European countries, but never respectable in American politics, it seems arguable that Britain is more closely linked in its political roots to Europe than to the US.

The question, however, is not just whether European countries are recognisably 'European', but whether their recognisably European characteristics are likely to make a decisive difference in terms of economic outcomes. And the specific question facing our enquiry is whether these recognisably European characteristics are likely to produce decisively worse outcomes in terms of employment and unemployment; and in that respect, therefore, whether the social outcomes are also likely to be worse.

The problem is that at the level of practical detail, as opposed to broad generality, the European countries are in many cases quite different from each other, in their political systems, in their economic structures, in their social systems. As a result, they respond rather differently to the new challenges of globalisation and structural and technological change, and consequently some of them are proving significantly more successful than others in meeting these challenges.

It is not surprising, therefore, that these differences also show up in the unemployment figures. Free-enterprise critics of the 'Rhineland Model' sometimes seem to imply that high unemployment is a natural if not inevitable consequence of the short-comings of the characteristic European system. In fact, however, unemployment levels in Europe are extraordinarily varied, from very high to very low, and in a significant proportion of European countries, unemployment is or has been lower than in the United States. In addition, national governments often define their unemployment figures in different terms from the internationally recognised norms.

In 1996, unemployment was in double figures in eight west European countries, including Germany (10.3 per cent), France (12.4) and Italy (12.1), whereas it was only 5.4 per cent in the US. But the spread of unemployment in western Europe in that year ranged from 3.3 per cent in Luxembourg, 4.3 per cent in Iceland and 4.7 per cent in Switzerland, up to 13.1 per cent in Belgium, 16.3 per cent in Finland and 22.7 per cent in Spain.

Some of these one-year figures inevitably reflect in part cyclical factors or the effects of short-term shocks. But if one takes average figures over a longer period, so as to smooth out these elements and show up the influence of structural factors, one still gets a rather wide range of results. Wide enough, in fact, to raise at least a question mark over the notion, in its simplest form, that the 'Rhineland' model is inevitably associated with high unemployment.

Over the period 1989-94, when average US unemployment was 6.2 per cent, nine countries in western Europe had higher unemployment, including Spain (18.9 per cent), Ireland (14.8), France (10.4) and Britain (8.9); but six countries had lower unemployment, including the quintessentially Rhineland Germany (5.4 per cent), Austria (3.7) and Switzerland (2.3).

Over an earlier period 1983-88, when average US unemployment was 7.1 per cent, eight countries in western Europe had higher unemployment, again including Spain (19.6 per cent), Ireland (16.1), Britain (10.9) and France (9.8), but seven had lower unemployment, again including Germany (6.8 per cent), Austria (3.6) and Switzerland (0.8).

And over the whole period 1983-96, when average US unemployment was 6.5 per cent, nine countries in western Europe had higher unemployment, again including Spain (19.7 per cent), Ireland (15.1), France (10.4) and Britain (9.7); but six had lower unemployment, again including Germany (6.2 per cent), Austria (3.8) and Switzerland (1.8).

Table One: Unemployment Rates in the OECD

	1983-96	1983-88			1989-94		
	Total	Total	Short-term	Long-term	Total	Short-term	Long-term
Austria	3.8	3.6	-	-	3.7	-	-
Belgium	9.7	11.3	3.3	8.0	8.1	2.9	5.1
Denmark	9.9	9.0	6.0	3.0	10.8	7.9	3.0
Finland	9.1	5.1	4.0	1.0	10.5	8.9	1.7
France	10.4	9.8	5.4	4.4	10.4	6.5	3.9
W.Germany	6.2	6.8	3.7	3.1	5.4	3.2	2.2
Ireland	15.1	16.1	6.9	9.2	14.8	5.4	9.4
Italy	7.6	6.9	3.1	3.8	8.2	2.9	5.3
Netherlands	8.4	10.5	5.0	5.5	7.0	3.5	3.5
Norway	4.2	2.7	2.5	0.2	5.5	4.3	1.2
Portugal	6.4	7.6	3.5	4.2	5.0	3.0	2.0
Spain	19.7	19.6	8.3	11.3	18.9	9.1	9.7
Sweden	4.3	2.6	2.3	0.3	4.4	4.0	0.4
Switzerland	1.8	0.8	0.7	0.1	2.3	1.8	0.5
UK	9.7	10.9	5.8	5.1	8.9	5.5	3.4
Canada	9.8	9.9	9.0	0.9	9.8	8.9	0.9
USA	6.5	7.1	6.4	0.7	6.2	5.6	0.6
Japan	2.6	2.7	0.5	2.2	2.3	0.4	1.9
Australia	8.7	8.4	2.4	5.9	9.0	2.7	6.2
New Zealand	6.8	4.9	0.6	4.3	8.9	2.3	6.6

Source: Nickell, *Journal of Economic Perspectives*, 1997

What is striking is the comparative constancy of the figures for these earlier periods, in terms of the relative rankings of some of the European countries vis-à-vis the US and vis-à-vis each other. This constancy may suggest that there could be some constant factors at work in some of the European countries. But the results are so different between different European countries, that it seems logical to infer that there may be different constant factors at work in different European countries.

It certainly seems difficult to argue that a single group of constant factors — the 'Rhineland Model', for example — could be responsible for such a wide range of different results between different European countries.

It seems even more difficult to argue that it is the 'Rhineland Model' which explains the fact that unemployment is today much higher in Germany than the US, in view of the fact that unemployment used to be consistently much lower in Germany than the US for a sustained stretch of years as recently as the 1970s and 1980s. For if there is any validity in the concept of the 'Rhineland Model' (and there may be), it surely implies a model which is fairly deeply-rooted and stable over time. In which case, similar causes must produce similar effects.

So it is surely necessary to look in more detail at some of the disaggregated factors operating in the economies of Europe and America.

3. Europe and America

Despite considerable progress over the past three to four decades, Europe still lags behind the US in terms of both level of productivity and level of employment.

As the European Commission's Annual Economic Report for 1997 states: 'The labour productivity growth performance of the Community has resulted in a steady catching-up with the productivity level of the United States. The economy-wide Community productivity level (on a purchasing-power-standard basis) relative to the United States increased from 45 per cent in 1960 to 82 per cent in 1995. However, over this period, the Community did not succeed in narrowing the gap in living standards with the United States to a similar degree. GDP per head of population relative to the United States increased from 55 per cent in 1960 to only 71 per cent in 1995'.

Europe's problem is that, while its rate of productivity improvement in Europe has been much greater than in the US — averaging close to 2 per cent a year since the mid-1970s compared with well under one per cent a year in the US — its employment growth has been much less. As the Commission report says: 'Apart from the growth period of the second half of the 1980s, the rate of job creation has been too slow and below the comparatively modest rise in the labour force. The United States, by contrast, has enjoyed rapid employment growth since the early 1960s, broadly in tandem with a strong increase in the labour force. As a result, the two regions experienced opposite trends in the employment ratio. Starting from a level somewhat below that in the Community, the employment rate in the United States rose to around 73 per cent at present whereas it declined to below 60 per cent in the Community'.

The difference in the employment rate between the EU and the US — equivalent to some 35 million jobs in Europe, double the number recorded as unemployed — has substantially offset the benefits of having achieved higher rates of growth of productivity per worker in Europe.

The second problem, as noted in a 1997 report on *The Competitiveness of European Industry* published by the Commission's Directorate-General for Industry, is that taxation is much higher in

Europe than in the US (or Japan), and has increased substantially in recent years.

Between 1970 and 1995, the tax take as a share of GDP went up from 34 per cent to 43 per cent in the European Union, whereas in the US it rose by a much smaller amount from a lower base, from 28 per cent to 30 per cent. In addition, indirect taxes and social security contributions are significantly higher in Europe than in the US (or Japan), and the effective tax rate on labour employed rose in Europe on average between 1980 and 1994 from 34 per cent to 40 per cent.

Nominal labour costs have long risen faster in Europe than in the US, though the rate of increase has been decelerating. But after taking account of inflation, real labour costs are rising more slowly in Europe than in the US: by 0.7 per cent per annum in 1990-95, compared with 1.2 per cent p.a. in the US.

In European manufacturing industry, however, labour costs increased faster than in the economy as a whole. Productivity has also gone up in Europe, but less than in the US, so that in the period 1990-95 unit labour costs in European manufacturing industry have been rising by 0.5 per cent faster per annum than the in US. On the other hand, the principal US achievement is not mainly in productivity, but in job creation: in some European countries, productivity per hour worked is higher than in the US, though the number of hours worked is lower.

Although total labour costs account for 70 per cent of GDP in both the US and Europe, the structure of labour costs can also be important for employment, particularly at the lower end of the labour market. The *Competitiveness* report comments that non-wage labour costs make up 44 per cent of labour costs in the European Union, compared to 28 per cent in the US (and 24 per cent in Japan). 'Employers' social contributions in most Member States are regressive, that is, they do not increase in line with wages. This effectively sets a floor on labour costs in most European countries. Thus the structure of taxes and social security contributions is such that their relative burden is generally heavier on low-paid workers. This category of workers, where unemployment is disproportionately high, is also that for which the price variable tends to play a greater role in hiring decisions'.

Free-market critics of the Rhineland Model often emphasise what they see as the excessive regulation of European labour markets. But the Commission report points out that the degree of labour market flexibility does not only stem from labour market regulation per se. In fact, it argues, the main limitations on growth and employment appear to come from restrictions on access to other markets, such as company pension schemes or rigidities in the housing market.

This last point is strongly echoed in a recent report by McKinsey called *Removing Barriers to Growth and Employment in France and Germany.*

The main barriers to growth and productivity in these two countries, the study claims, are sector-specific product market regulations, such as zoning laws, or excessively high minimum wages. The negative impact of such restrictions is particularly pronounced in retailing, it found. In France, for example, the high minimum wage has effectively led to 15 per cent lower employment than in the US in comparable retail outlets. Conversely, the study found that minimum wage costs in the US in 1995 were about 55 per cent of the French level, and that 26 per cent of labour in the US is employed below the level of official French minimum wage costs.

The Commission's report on *The Competitiveness of European Industry* points out that, contrary to conventional wisdom, European labour markets are as dynamic as that of the US, though the high levels of job turnover in Europe are not matched by the rate of net job creation. The obstacles to job creation, it says, may take many forms, including wage bargaining systems, restrictions on working times, and employment protection legislation. In the US (and Japan) wage bargaining characteristically takes place at plant level, whereas in continental Europe the dominant mode has been sector-wide bargaining, though in the 1980s and 1990s there has been a trend towards more de-centralised bargaining. But the report says that it is not possible to conclude that any one form of bargaining is inherently superior.

In recent years, says the report, there has been a relaxation of labour market regulation in Europe. Virtually all Member States have seen a significant reduction in working time regulations, and recruitment restrictions have been relaxed. It has become easier for employers to take on part-time as well as temporary workers, and the possibilities for self-employment have increased considerably.

But the Commission's report points out that inflexibility may come as much from attitudes as from legislation. Working hours are much shorter in the European Union, at 1,643 hours per annum compared with 1,940 in the US. And a significant proportion of European companies have had difficulty in finding workers willing to work on Saturdays, despite the high levels of unemployment.

4. The Labour Market

The conventional wisdom is that many European countries have very high unemployment, whereas the US does not, because the job markets in Europe are rigid, inflexible and regulated, whereas the American labour market is deregulated and free. This view certainly corresponds with the analysis of the OECD (see below).

The most obvious general contrast between Europe and America, in this context, is that America is a single labour market, whereas Europe is a series of national labour markets effectively compartmentalised by language and culture, and still, to some extent, by national legislation. But in addition, there is much more regional mobility in America than in most European countries. In the US, about 3 per cent of households change their region of residence in a year, whereas in Britain, Germany and France the figure is closer to 1 per cent, and is even lower in Italy and Spain.

This low level of regional mobility in Europe may be aggravated by higher levels of unemployment, and it is regularly cited by critics as one of the structural reasons for questioning the viability of the project for Economic and Monetary Union in Europe. For if economic adjustment can no longer take place through the exchange rate, once national currencies have been replaced by a single European currency, then it would need to take place in other ways, for example by labour mobility.

In Norway and Sweden, however, regional mobility has always been an objective of labour market policy, and regional mobility rates in those two countries are comparable with the US; it also happens that unemployment has consistently been low in Norway, and also (until recently) in Sweden.

But beyond the very broad contrasts between Europe and America, it quickly becomes clear that there is great diversity between the national labour markets in Europe, in terms of how they are affected by legislation and regulation, by the treatment of unemployment, by the role of unions, or by the taxation of labour.

In one recent study, Professor Stephen Nickell of Oxford has re-examined the conventional wisdom about Europe's inflexible labour markets, and he has concluded it is too vague and too sweeping to be useful. For though there are features of some European labour markets which do indeed help sustain high unemployment, and some of them can be characterised as rigidities, there are other so-called rigidities which do not cause unemployment, and may even serve a useful purpose.

As a first step to breaking down the diversity of national labour markets, Professor Nickell has set out indicators of ten different aspects of these markets, ranging from direct hire-and-fire legislation to the incidence of payroll taxation.

Employment protection

The employment protection index, drawn up by the OECD, ranks the member states from 1 to 20, according to whether hiring and firing is strictly regulated or not.

The United States ranks number 1, i.e. its labour market is the least regulated, while Italy at number 20 is the most regulated. Within Europe, the other most heavily regulated labour markets are in Mediterranean or quasi-Mediterranean countries, Spain (19) and Portugal (18); while the least regulated countries are more northerly: Denmark (5), Switzerland (6) and UK (7). But France (14), Germany (15) and Austria (16) are all towards the more regulated end of the scale.

Some features of this ranking seem to correspond with the conventional wisdom, at least in terms of today's situation: Germany currently has a heavily regulated labour market, and it also has spectacularly high unemployment, whereas Britain has a very unregulated labour market, and steadily falling unemployment.

The trouble with this logical correspondence is that it is a recent innovation: Germany has always had a rather regulated labour market, whereas Britain has always had a very unregulated labour market; but until a few years ago, Germany generally had low unemployment, while Britain generally had high unemployment.

Labour standards

The OECD has also drawn up a labour standards index, which scores countries on other aspects of the labour market: such as working time, fixed-term contracts, employment protection, minimum wages, and representation rights. Each of these five dimensions is scored from 0 (lax or no legislation) to 2 (strict legislation), with resulting composite scores which range from 0 (very unregulated) to 10 (very regulated).

The least regulated labour markets are in the US and the UK, both of which score 0, and the most regulated are Italy, Spain and Sweden (7

Table Two: Features of Labour Markets 1 (1989-94)

	Employment Protection	Labour Standards	Benefit Replacement Rate (%)	Benefit Duration (years)	Active Labour Market Policies
Austria	16	5	50	2	8.3
Belgium	17	4	60	4	14.6
Denmark	5	2	90	2.5	10.3
Finland	10	5	63	2	16.4
France	14	6	57	3	8.8
W.Germany	15	6	63	4	25.7
Ireland	12	4	37	4	9.1
Italy	20	7	20	0.5	10.3
Netherlands	9	5	70	2	6.9
Norway	11	5	65	1.5	14.7
Portugal	18	4	65	0.8	18.8
Spain	19	7	70	3.5	4.7
Sweden	13	7	80	1.2	59.3
Switzerland	6	3	70	1	8.2
UK	7	0	38	4	6.4
Canada	3	2	59	1	5.9
USA	1	0	50	0.5	3.0
Japan	8	1	60	0.5	4.3
Australia	4	3	36	4	3.2
New Zealand	2	3	30	4	6.8

Source: Nickell, Journal of Economic Perspectives, 1997

each). But France and Germany are almost as regulated, with scores of 6 each, while Denmark (2) and Switzerland (3) are at the unregulated end of the scale.

Unemployment benefit

Professor Nickell has set out figures indicating the relative generosity of the unemployment benefit systems in the member states; both in terms of the 'replacement rate' (that is, the value of unemployment benefit as a proportion of previous earned income), and of how long the unemployed are eligible for benefit. Here Italy is the least generous, with a replacement

Table Three: Features of Labour Markets II (1989-94)

	Union Density (%)	Union Coverage Index	Union Coordination	Employer Coordination	Payroll Tax Rate (%)	Total Tax rate (%)
Austria	46.2	3	3	3	22.6	53.7
Belgium	51.2	3	2	2	21.5	49.8
Denmark	71.4	3	3	3	0.6	46.3
Finland	72.0	3	2	3	25.5	65.9
France	9.8	3	2	2	38.8	63.8
W.Germany	32.9	3	2	3	23.0	53.0
Ireland	49.7	3	1	1	7.1	34.3
Italy	38.8	3	2	2	40.2	62.9
Netherlands	25.5	3	2	2	27.5	56.5
Norway	56.0	3	3	3	17.5	48.6
Portugal	31.8	3	2	2	14.5	37.6
Spain	11.0	3	2	1	33.2	54.2
Sweden	82.5	3	3	3	37.8	70.7
Switzerland	26.6	2	1	3	14.5	38.6
UK	39.1	2	1	1	13.8	40.8
Canada	35.8	2	1	1	13.0	42.7
USA	15.6	1	1	1	20.9	43.8
Japan	25.4	2	2	2	16.5	36.3
Australia	40.4	3	2	1	2.5	28.7
New Zealand	44.8	2	1	1	-	34.8

Source: Nickell, Journal of Economic Perspectives, 1997

rate of 20 per cent, for a maximum of six months, followed by the US (50 per cent, for six months); whereas the most generous are Belgium, Denmark, Germany and Spain.

Active labour market policies

The figures for Active Labour Market Policies (ALMPs) indicate how much effort governments are making actively to get the unemployed back into work, and are measured in terms of government spending on such activities as training, job search and job creation. The Swedes are far ahead of all other countries, since their spending on ALMPs for each unemployed person, is equivalent to nearly 60 per cent of national output per worker. By contrast, Spain and the UK spend very little on ALMPs, nearly as little as the US.

The role of trades unions

The next four sets of figures indicate the relative importance of trades unions and the role they play in setting wages. They show that union membership in the US is very low, at less than 16 per cent of the work force. But even though union membership is nominally even lower in Spain (11 per cent) and France (9.8), operatively the unions still play a leading role in those two countries, since they negotiate on behalf of over 70 per cent of the work force. In Austria, Denmark, Norway and Sweden, wage negotiations are conducted with a great deal of co-ordination between unions and employers; in Britain, Ireland and the US there is very little co-ordination.

Payroll and other taxes

Payroll taxes vary widely, from Denmark (almost zero) to France and Italy (close to 40 per cent of wages). But total tax takes, including payroll, income and consumption taxes, vary less, from 34.3 per cent in Ireland to 70.7 per cent in Sweden.

When Professor Nickell performed time-series calculations on these ten indicators of the different aspects of the labour market function, and of the statistical relationship between them and unemployment, he came up with some unexpected or at least counter-intuitive results.

Labour standards

First, he found no statistical correlation between high labour standards and overall unemployment; and yet employment protection would, damagingly, tend to increase long-term unemployment, while tending at the same time to reduce short-term unemployment.

Unemployment benefit and active labour market policies

Generous unemployment benefit systems tend to lead to high unemployment, and long-term benefits tend to generate long-term unemployment. Conversely, if unemployment benefit is not long-term, ALMPs can be effective in reducing unemployment, especially long-term unemployment.

Role of the unions

Powerful trades unions tend to be able to raise pay faster than productivity, and therefore to increase unemployment. But this effect is counteracted if unions and employers coordinate their negotiations, because this prevents leap-frogging.

Payroll taxes

The OECD and others frequently argue in favour of reducing payroll taxes, on the grounds that a payroll tax is a tax on jobs. But in fact it appears that the key tax rate for the labour market is not the payroll tax, but the combined weight of payroll tax, income tax, and consumption taxes. If the balance of the tax burden is simply shifted from payroll tax to consumption taxes, the evidence is that this will have no long-run impact on unemployment. But an increase in the total tax burden may tend to increase unemployment.

Minimum wages

It appears that minimum wages tend to be too low to affect the employment of adult men, but have a significant though small adverse effect on youth unemployment.

Unemployment of the unskilled

It is often argued that there has been a significant shift in demand from unskilled to skilled workers; that in Europe this has translated into higher unemployment, as a result of the rigidity of Europe's labour markets and wage-setting systems; but that in the US it has translated into more wage inequality (i.e. relative wage-cutting at the bottom), because of the flexibility of the American labour market.

According to Professor Nickell, the evidence suggests that skill shifts account for at most 20 per cent of the rise in unemployment in Europe since the 1970s. While this affects a large number of people and underlines the importance of raising the level of skills in many European countries, and in Britain in particular, it is far from explaining the difference between Europe and the US. Moreover, unskilled unemployment has risen in the US by over 100 per cent since the 1970s, despite the fall in unskilled real wages.

In any case, the impact of the decline in demand for unskilled workers is much mitigated in countries where training and education are most effective in raising the capability of the least well-endowed; notably Austria, Germany, Holland, Switzerland and Scandinavia.

In the last analysis, Professor Nickell concludes that high unemployment is associated with four labour market features:

(a) general unemployment benefits which run on indefinitely; and low levels of active policies to stimulate the return to work;

(b) high unionisation, but without co-ordination in wage bargaining;

(c) high tax burden and high minimum wages for young people;

(d) poor educational standards at the bottom of the labour market.

Conversely, he believes there are three labour market features which do not seem to push up overall unemployment:

(a) strict employment protection laws and high labour market standards, even if they do tend to increase long-term unemployment;

(b) generous unemployment benefit, provided it is limited in time and backed by active labour market policies.

(c) high unionisation, if combined with co-ordination in wage bargaining, especially among employers.

In other words, his conclusions suggest that it is not the essential characteristics of the Rhineland Model which are to blame for Europe's current ills, but quite detailed defects in the way they are implemented.

5. The International Context

In the section on the Labour Market, we considered the argument that Europe's high mass unemployment can be largely blamed on the rigidities of Europe's labour markets. In this section, we shall consider the much more sweeping claim that Europe's problems derive not just from rigidities in the labour markets, but much more broadly from over-regulation throughout the economy.

For it is commonly said by free-market critics that the recent rise in mass unemployment is a general wake-up call to Europe, indicating that the 'Rhineland Model', with all its inherited traditions of corporatism and regulation, is a serious handicap in the increasingly competitive world of global markets and rapid structural change. They argue that all the typically European baggage of consensus, negotiation, regulation and social solidarity, not just in labour markets, but right across the board, will have to be swept away if the European economies are to be able to compete with America, Japan and the tiger economies of Asia.

On the face of it, this seems a logical point of view. The American economy is in general much more deregulated than the economies of Europe; America has for several years been enjoying low unemployment and high economic growth; Europe has for several years been suffering from high mass unemployment and low economic growth; ergo, Europe must become more like America.

But a different analysis is also possible: yes, European economies are in many ways too regulated and protectionist, and should be deregulated; but no, economic regulation is not the primary reason for the rise in unemployment.

Economic growth

Instead, some analysts argue that the primary reason for high unemployment in Europe is that economic growth has been too low to sustain employment; and that one of the principal contributory factors in Europe's low economic growth has been economic mismanagement, notably by the German Bundesbank.

This is certainly the point of view argued in a major recent analysis of international trends in growth and employment, published last year by the Deutsches Institut für Wirtschaftsforschung (DIW) of Berlin. The study, which was carried out for the Social Affairs Ministry of the Netherlands government, was designed to investigate the employment and social policies of OECD countries; and to see whether the internationalisation of the world economy will make it more difficult for governments to implement national employment and social policies.

Their conclusion was that the rise in unemployment in Europe has not been caused primarily by rigidities in Europe's labour markets, but mainly by successive macro-economic shocks: the oil-price shocks of the 1970s, the deflation of the early 1980s, and the recession of 1992-93.

In the last analysis, the study found, the most decisive factor influencing employment is economic growth: Europe has higher unemployment than the US essentially because in recent years it has had significantly lower economic growth.

And one of the most important reasons for this, it concluded, is that the Federal Reserve has been much more successful in fine tuning monetary policy for growth in the US, than the Bundesbank has been in Germany for Europe, because the Bundesbank has been too cautious in pursuing anti-inflationary policies too long and too hard.

But, if unemployment is to be brought down in Europe, it will not be enough just to secure a growth rate averaging 2-3 per cent over the whole business cycle; in addition, the economic upswings will have to be long and the downturns short. For it seems to be a feature of the unemployment pattern in Europe, that it is much quicker to rise than to fall again: once unemployment has risen in response to a severe recession, it tends to remain durably higher.

'There is a substantial danger', says the DIW study, 'that the European economy gets permanently stuck on a low-growth path with hardly reversible consequences for the level of employment'.

The study finds that Europe's unemployment problems have no doubt been aggravated by defects in its labour market mechanisms and policies. In particular, the stickiness of unemployment in Europe has been accentuated by the fact that many European countries had (and still have) generous and loosely-administered unemployment benefit systems, (which helped sustain unemployment), and inadequate active labour market policies for getting the unemployed back to work. But these defects are essentially secondary to the main problem, of inadequate economic growth.

But the study gives short shrift to the widespread idea that Europe's welfare states are no longer competitive in an age of increasing competition from low-wage countries, pointing out that while a highly developed welfare state may cause incentive problems, international trade is not based on competition between nations, but between industries.

Internationalisation

Moreover, the DIW team contests the conventional idea that the internationalisation of the world economy is dramatically accelerating. Certainly, the internationalisation of manufacturing industry has continued rather rapidly: since 1970-72, the exposure of OECD manufacturing sectors to foreign trade, as measured by exports as a share of production, and imports as a share of consumption, has grown from around 25 per cent to around 40 per cent.

But this internationalisation of manufacturing has taken place in parallel with the continued relative shift away from manufacturing towards services, where exposure to foreign trade is much lower (around 5-6 per cent on average) and virtually static. As a result, the overall level of exposure to international trade has grown much more modestly for the total economies of the OECD countries than for their manufacturing sectors alone; from around 12 per cent on average in 1970-72 to 15-16 per cent in 1991-93. In Germany, of course, the share of manufacturing is larger than in many other OECD countries, so its exposure to international trade is also correspondingly larger.

On the other hand, the study is clear that the internationalisation of the world economy has shifted, and will continue to shift, the balance of advantage against the unskilled workers in the industrialised world. They will be the main losers from the effects of globalisation and structural change, while the main winners will be savers, innovative entrepreneurs, and skilled workers.

One of the striking indicators of this shift can be seen in Britain and America, where labour markets and wage rates are least regulated, and where inequalities of earnings have widened steadily since at least the beginning of the 1980s. One standard measure of earnings inequality is the ratio between the bottom of the top 10 per cent of wage earners, and the top of the bottom 10 per cent of wage earners. And by this measure, earnings inequality in the US has risen from a ratio of 3.5 in 1982 to 4.3 in the mid-1990s; and in Britain over the same period from 2.7 to 3.7. In continental Europe, by contrast, wage inequality has generally remained constant, or even in some countries (Germany and Belgium) actually declined.

Free-market critics of the 'Rhineland Model' sometimes argue as if there were a simple trade-off between inequality and unemployment. In both Europe and America, they say, the odds have tilted against the unskilled workers. But America has preferred to deal with the problem by wage flexibility, which secures lower unemployment, if at the cost of some (possibly temporary) inequality; whereas Europe has preferred to resist wage inequality through its regulated labour markets, but at the cost of higher unemployment.

The DIW study absolutely rejects this argument. For it would imply that more of the unskilled are priced back into the labour market in the US and the UK, than in continental Europe. In fact, however, the unemployment rates of unskilled workers were significantly higher in Britain and America in 1992 than in Germany, the Netherlands or the OECD average.

Moreover youth unemployment, too, is significantly higher in Britain and America than Germany, Japan or Denmark. And this, it says, may point to an explanation for the fact that Britain and America have higher unemployment among the unskilled: less good basic education, less good vocational training, and less on-the-job training. And in fact, the comparison of skill levels supports this view: in 1991, 61 per cent of employees in the UK were low- or un-skilled workers, while the corresponding rates were much lower in Germany (16 per cent), Denmark (28) or the Netherlands (37).

The question of the unskilled, and the comparison between Europe and America, is discussed further in the section on Germany.

Capital mobility

One of the corollaries of the shift against unskilled labour, in the internationalisation of the world economy, is likely to be a shift in favour of capital. And since capital is increasingly mobile and foot-loose, the process of internationalisation would seem to imply increasing competition between countries in their efforts to attract foreign direct investment (FDI).

Some analysts deduce that this process will involve competitive tax-cutting between states, and will lead to the impoverishment of national tax bases, and thus to increasing constraints on national spending policies, especially on social policies. But the DIW study takes a more optimistic view, arguing that competition for FDI could even promote government spending on socially useful policies.

Table Four: Structure of Unemployment, 1983 and 1985 (per cent)

Source: DIW, Unemployment & Social Policies

	Unemployment		Employment		Total labour market slack		Long-term unemployment		Youth unemployment		Women's unemployment		Unskilled unemployment	
	1983	1995	1983	1995	1983	1993	1983	1995	1983	1995	1983	1995	1983	1992
Germany	7.7	8.2	62.2	65.1	(7.4)	(8.5)	41.6	48.3	11.0	8.5	8.8	9.8		8.9
UK	12.4	8.7	64.3	67.8	13.3	12.5	45.6	43.5	19.7	15.5	11.5	4.3		12.3
Japan	2.6	3.1	71.1	74.1	6.8	5.7	12.9	18.1	4.5	6.1	2.6	3.2		-
USA	9.5	5.5	66.2	73.5	13.9	10.2	13.3	9.7	17.2	12.1	9.2	5.6		13.5
Netherlands	12.0	6.5	52.1	64.3	-	10.6	48.8	43.2	24.9	13.1	12.9	7.1		8.0
Belgium	12.1	9.4	54.6	55.7	12.8	11.4	64.8	62.4	23.9	21.5	17.8	10.8		13.0
Denmark	10.4	10.1	71.7	73.4	11.3	14.7	44.3	27.9	18.9	9.9	10.4	11.1		15.6
Sweden	3.9	9.2	78.5	71.1	-	10.2	10.3	15.7	8.0	15.4	3.6	6.9		4.6
Average	8.8	7.6	65.1	68.1	10.9	10.5	35.2	33.6	16.0	12.8	9.6	7.4		10.8

According to a widely held opinion, capital will tend to flow to countries with lower tax rates. As a result, it is argued, countries will tend to reduce their taxation of capital, and therefore capital (and other mobile factors) will tend to be taxed less and less, while immobile factors of production, such as labour or land, as well as various types of consumption, will tend to be taxed more and more.

So it seems to prove, up to a point. The tax burden on companies has been lightened in most industrial countries during the past decade. In Britain, taxes on profits have come down substantially since the early 1980s, while in Germany a smaller reduction in taxes on profits has been accompanied by an increase in taxes on wages and social security contributions.

The reduction in corporation tax rates has been especially marked in those countries which previously had high rates of taxation; so the spread of corporate tax rates has been reduced noticeably across industrial countries. As a result, there is concern in some European countries, which is shared by the Commission, that the European Union needs to take steps to avoid a tax-cutting war in Europe.

However, the DIW team do not expect any race for the lowest tax rate in the next few years, partly because they believe that flows of FDI will be influenced not just by tax rates, but by the quality of the immobile factors of production in the host country. Therefore they argue that the promotion of these immobile factors of production — human capital in the form of education and training, basic research capabilities, and physical and transport infrastructure — will become an increasingly important task of economic and social policy. Countries well supplied with internationally immobile factors of production will also be good locations for physical investment as well as the development and application of technology.

Macro-economic policy

Since the first oil shock in 1974, public spending deficits in most OECD countries have substantially deteriorated, mostly because of recession-related expenditures, but also as a result of rising health and pension costs. As a result, the burden of debt service has generally become much heavier, aggravated by the rise in unemployment in most European countries.

In many countries the debt burden has now become unsustainable, and its stabilisation and reduction of public debt will increasingly be given political priority. But in many countries this can only be achieved within a reasonable time-frame — say two decades — if they run a primary budget surplus (that is, not counting debt service) of at least 5 per cent of GDP.

This, according to the DIW study, will have two consequences. First, the role of fiscal policy in macro-economic management will be much reduced, with the result that monetary policy will have to play a bigger role. Second, the scope for public spending will be substantially constrained, especially no doubt in the case of social policies.

As it is, DIW believes monetary policy already plays the central role in macro-economic management, and identifies the contrast in performance between the Federal Reserve in the US and the Bundesbank in Germany, as the key factor explaining the difference in economic performance between the US and Europe.

Monetary policy

In the US, the Fed started exerting a dominant influence on the business cycle after the mid-1980s, according to DIW, and was mainly responsible both for the recession of 1990/91 and for the subsequent recovery of 1991/92.

'Thanks to its impressive record of fighting inflation since the early 1980s', says the study, 'the Fed enjoys immense credibility and thus wields considerable influence over expectations. People anticipate low inflation and are therefore willing to accept a lower rise in wages.' As a result, the problems connected with price-stabilisation-induced recessions can be avoided.

In Germany, by contrast, the Bundesbank has concentrated too much and too often on suppressing inflation, to the disregard of the promotion of economic growth; or else there has been insufficient co-ordination between the monetary policy of the Bundesbank and the fiscal policy of the government.

As a result of what the DIW team perceives as the Bundesbank's excessive concern with the dangers of inflation, the German economy got durably stuck on a lower growth path, with a lower level of employment. Moreover, they say, the general failures of German economic policy, and in particular the excessive deflationary effects of German monetary policy, have also had adverse repercussions in the rest of Europe, not just among the West European members of the European Monetary System (EMS), but also in Eastern Europe.

Social solidarity

The key dilemma for social policy in Europe, according to the DIW analysis, follows on from the public debt crisis inherited by many governments from the 1980s.

On the one hand, the central social problem in coming years will be the widening of economic equalities, because market forces are likely to lead to a further decline in real incomes of low-skilled workers relative to skilled workers, as has already happened in the US and the UK. Moreover, increasing capital mobility will raise the income of savers, but erode the options for taxation of capital. But on the other hand, governments' fiscal room for manoeuvre, to be able to counteract these inequalities through spending policies, will be severely constrained by their need to reduce the level of debt by primary budget surpluses.

'The ultimate constraint on social policy', the DIW report concludes, 'will not be internationalisation, but the consensus prevailing in a society on how much income inequality should be tolerated. Whether internationalisation will benefit all workers in OECD countries depends on the willingness of the winners to compensate the losers. At least in some countries, there is increasing evidence that they are unwilling to do so.'

Other analysts would argue, on the contrary, that internationalisation will be the ultimate constraint on social policy, because it will expose the problems of the social system and of the economy in Europe: the fundamental test is whether Europe can meet the competitive challenge of the global economy.

Either way, however, the clear implication is that, in the absence of far-reaching reforms, internationalisation is likely to represent an increasing challenge to the values of social solidarity embedded in the Rhineland Model.

6. The OECD Jobs Study

In 1994, in response to the rising tide of mass unemployment, the OECD launched its *Jobs Strategy*, with a list of ten recommended reforms intended to promote employment in the member states.

Since then, it has systematically monitored the fate of its recommendations, and has conducted regular reviews of the performance of the member states in carrying them out.

Needless to say, the OECD does not officially recognise the existence of the Rhineland Model or indeed any other heterodox socio-economic model. For one thing, that would be bad politics for a multilateral organisation; for another, the OECD's natural creed is that what is good for some is good for all, and it starts with an orthodox free-market prejudice in favour of liberalism and deregulation.

And yet when the member states have discussed the *Jobs Strategy* and the recommended reforms, at the OECD headquarters at the Château de la Muette in Paris, it is clear that their debates have at times reflected explicit and profound disagreements over whether the priority should be deregulation and free markets, or equity and social solidarity.

It is clear, because the OECD has been unusually explicit in describing these political disagreements, in its latest assessment of the interim state of the Jobs Strategy: *Lessons from Member Countries' Experience*, published earlier this year.

These were the ten recommendations of the OECD in 1994:

1. Set macro-economic policy such that it will both encourage growth and, in conjunction with good structural policies, make it sustainable, i.e. non-inflationary.

2. Enhance the creation and diffusion of technological know-how by improving the frameworks for its development.

3. Increase flexibility of working time (both short-term and lifetime) voluntarily sought by workers and employers.

4. Nurture an entrepreneurial climate by eliminating impediments to, and restrictions on, the creation and expansion of enterprises.

5. Make wage and labour costs more flexible by removing restrictions that prevent wages from reflecting local conditions and individual skill levels, in particular of younger workers.

6. Reform employment security provisions that inhibit the expansion of employment in the private sector.

7. Strengthen the emphasis on active labour market policies and reinforce their effectiveness.

8. Improve labour force skills and competences through wide-ranging changes in education and training systems.

9. Reform unemployment and related benefit systems — and their interactions with the tax system — such that societies' fundamental equity goals are achieved in ways that impinge far less on the efficient functioning of the labour markets.

10. Enhance production market competition so as to reduce monopolistic tendencies and weaken insider-outsider mechanisms while also contributing to a more innovative and dynamic economy.

It appears that the OECD, like the DIW institute, gives the first priority to the promotion of economic growth. But it may be observed that four of the ten recommendations (numbers 3, 5, 6 and 9) are part of the standard free-market preoccupation with the deregulation of labour markets.

The central judgment of the OECD's of *Lessons from Member Countries' Experience* is that only four countries have really done well in introducing recommended reforms: Britain, Ireland, the Netherlands and New Zealand.

> 'A clear message from the review process is that governments, sometimes in concert with the social partners and taking due account of the specificities of each country, can introduce comprehensive reforms, along the line of the recommendations in the OECD Jobs Study, which will expand employment opportunities and reduce structural unemployment.
>
> 'However the reviews have revealed that only a few countries have introduced and sustained policy reforms in a sufficiently wide-ranging and consistent way to achieve such an improvement in labour market performance.'

The assessment reports that previously high structural unemployment has gone even higher in the 1990s in Spain, in Italy and, to a minor extent, in France. In Finland and Sweden structural unemployment has risen abruptly from previously low levels. In the large non-European countries (the US, Japan and Canada) structural unemployment has remained unchanged. But structural unemployment has fallen in Britain, Ireland, the Netherlands and New Zealand.

> 'The United Kingdom and New Zealand have pursued both wide-ranging and deep structural reforms, beginning already in the early to mid-1980s... Based on a more gradualist approach, the Netherlands has also pursued a comprehensive reform programme starting in the first half of the 1980s... In Ireland, macro-economic stabilisation began at the same time while structural changes commenced in the second half of the 1980s.
>
> 'The reform processes in these four countries share a number of common features. One is that they were all initiated at a time when serious economic disequilibria had made it clear that existing policies could no longer be sustained.
>
> 'Another is that all four countries put in place stability-oriented macro-economic frameworks focused on sound public finances and effective control of inflation. Even though the countries were not always successful in implementing these frameworks, by 1996 Ireland, the Netherlands and New Zealand combined inflation below 2 per cent with general government balances which were either in surplus (New Zealand) or had deficits of less than 3 per cent of GDP.'

But the OECD also emphasises that the reform processes were different in these four countries, reflecting their different starting positions.

- The Netherlands, which had had high labour costs, including very high payroll taxes, focused on achieving wage moderation through centralised bargaining and tax reductions, lowering minimum wages, especially for young workers, and scaling down payroll taxes especially on low-wage earners.

- The UK, with its history of troubled labour relations, gave priority to product market reform, privatisation and reform of labour law.

• New Zealand, which had been one of the most protectionist countries, gave priority to trade liberalisation and reduced government intervention.

• Ireland, with high unemployment, took action to reduce the generosity of unemployment benefits, cut marginal tax rates, and improve human capital formation.

Because of the different starting points of the different countries, the OECD says, it is difficult to draw strong, area-wide conclusions about specific reforms. But it finds that there is a broad contrast between those countries which adopted comprehensive reforms, and those which adopted a more piece-meal approach.

'Reforms in the UK, Canada, Australia, the Netherlands and New Zealand have typically affected very broad groups in the labour market, including those which may be characterised as 'insiders'.

'In contrast, reforms in some continental European countries, which have not been successful in bringing down structural unemployment, have often affected persons at the margin of the labour market but with very little impact on core groups.

• 'For example, instead of relaxing general employment protection provisions, some governments have preferred to introduce short-term contracts and liberalise employment protection for part-timers or workers in small firms (e.g. Germany, France, Belgium).

• 'Similarly, few countries have made large cuts to central parameters of unemployment benefit systems, such as replacement rates or the maximum duration of benefits, but many have tightened rules governing eligibility for benefits and controls on job-search behaviour'.

The central issue dividing the comprehensive reformers from the less comprehensive, says the OECD, is that the comprehensive reformers put a higher priority on deregulation while the others put a higher priority on equity and social cohesion.

The OECD argues that there is not necessarily a straight trade-off between labour market reform and social equity, especially when seen in a dynamic perspective. Nevertheless, it goes on:

'representatives from a number of countries considered that there was a trade-off between horizontal equity and employment objectives.

However representatives from other countries rejected the notion of a trade-off.

'Thus, representatives from some English-speaking countries saw low unemployment as an essential condition for, or element of, horizontal equity. And those from some continental European countries saw equity as a more fundamental goal than low unemployment.

Some countries, notably France, Belgium and the Nordic countries, according to the OECD, resist a wider distribution of wage rates as a means to reduce unemployment, and instead rely on government policies in education, training and active labour market measures to bring productivity levels into line with existing wage spreads. But the OECD comments tartly: 'It remains an open question whether a policy approach that sees public intervention in post-compulsory education, training and active labour market policies as a substitute for relative wage flexibility is effective, let alone cost-effective, particularly in a world of rapid structural change'.

Some countries, including France, Austria and Belgium have also argued in favour of a gradual and incremental reform, on the grounds that this would help preserve social cohesion. The OECD comments, with some acerbity: 'At the same time, however, high and persistent unemployment is itself likely to seriously impair social cohesion'.

But the OECD points out that a comprehensive reform programme need not imply a disregard for social cohesion. 'The Netherlands and Ireland are examples of countries introducing those policies through a consensual process, involving the social partners, and clearly not threatening social cohesion. And while the reform programmes in the United Kingdom and New Zealand were not implemented through a formal process of consensus, they have in fact met with considerable acceptance by the general public, as indicated by the fact that there is little political support for wholesale reversal of these reforms.'

But there was one crucial feature which was shared by these four countries, according to the OECD, and this was that specific reforms could be perceived as part of a broader strategy. Hence, reforms that affected particular groups may have met with less resistance because they were seen as part of an overall strategy affecting much wider groups, and thereby possessing an element of fairness.

Moreover, one of the conclusions of the OECD review process is that broad-based reform is likely to be more effective than localised reform, because of the effects of synergy.

Table Five: Structural Unemployment in the OECD

	1986	1990	1996
RISING			
Finland	5.5	8.0	15.4
Sweden	2.1	3.2	6.7
Germany	7.3	6.9	9.6
Iceland	0.8	1.5	3.8
Switzerland	0.7	1.3	3.1
Spain	19.1	19.8	20.9
Greece	6.7	7.0	8.0
Italy	8.4	9.7	10.6
Portugal	6.1	4.9	5.8
Austria	4.1	4.9	5.4
France	8.9	9.3	9.7
STABLE			
Norway	3.1	4.2	5.1
Australia	8.1	8.2	8.5
Japan	2.5	2.5	2.7
Turkey	7.5	7.6	7.5
United States	6.2	5.8	5.6
Belgium	11.7	10.8	10.6
Canada	8.3	9.0	8.5
Denmark	8.6	9.6	9.0
OECD average	*7.0*	*6.8*	*7.1*
FALLING			
Netherlands	8.0	7.0	6.3
New Zealand	4.7	7.3	6.0
UK	10.2	8.4	7.0
Ireland	15.3	16.0	12.8

Source: OECD, Implementing the Jobs Strategy, 1997

'First, pursuing a comprehensive approach to reform is likely to bring greater benefits than concentrating efforts in a few areas, even though the experience of the countries pursuing comprehensive reform suggests that the benefits of reform may still take a considerable time to show up.

'Second, comprehensive policy reform may ease some of the inherent policy trade-offs. By exposing wider segments of the population to structural reform, the process may be perceived as more fair, reducing strains on social cohesion'.

When *Lessons from Member Countries' Experience* was published in May 1997, it was the most authoritative expression of orthodoxy. But within a few months, OECD member governments were placing less emphasis, in their pre-occupations with the problem of unemployment, on deregulation and essentially market-oriented reforms, and more on concern with problems of social cohesion and social exclusion.

When OECD employment ministers met in Paris in October 1997, their main conclusion, in the final communiqué, was that: 'High and persistent unemployment and low pay affecting significant sections of the working age population risk becoming threats to the social fabric'.

The ministers said they were particularly concerned with high levels of youth unemployment. 'It is vital', they said, 'to reverse this situation for reasons of social cohesion and equity, and because young people represent an investment for the future'.

In addition, they expressed concern at the widening gaps, between the skilled and the unskilled, and between the well-paid and the low-paid.

'Low pay is an economic and social problem in its own right', they said. 'A low-paid job may be better than no job, and is often a stepping stone to a better job, especially among well-educated and trained youths. But others, especially women and workers with obsolete skills, and young people with low levels of education and work-related skills, get trapped in low-paid jobs or revolve between a low-paid job and no job altogether'.

7. Lessons from Britain

On the economic front today, Britain is a spectacular exception to the general scene of gloom in Europe. Most European governments lament the sluggish recovery from recession; the British government boasts of the vigour of the UK expansion. Unemployment in the European Union has been in double figures for five years, and shows little sign of coming down in any substantial way; in France, Italy and Belgium it is over 12 per cent, in Spain over 22 per cent. But in Britain unemployment has been falling for five years, and is expected to go on falling, according to the OECD, to under 6 per cent next year.

But there is a problem with comparing the unemployment levels in different countries, and it is that national governments use different definitions of unemployment. There is a widely recognised international definition of unemployment, used by the ILO and the OECD, which says that the unemployed are people of working age, who have no work, who are available for work, and who are actively looking for work. But this definition produces figures which may be different from national government figures.

In most cases, the differences are not great. In 1995, for instance, (the latest year for which the OECD has published unemployment figures under both national and international definitions), French unemployment was 11.5 per cent by the national definition, but 11.6 per cent by the ILO definition. Similarly, Italian unemployment in the same year was 12.0 per cent by the national definition, but 12.2 per cent by the ILO definition.

But in other cases the discrepancy can be quite substantial. In the case of Britain, for example, the national definition was modified many times by the previous Conservative government, always with the effect of reducing the officially declared rate of unemployment. In Germany, by contrast, the national definition produces figures which are larger than those derived from the international ILO/OECD definition.

So when British and German unemployment figures are translated into the standardised international definition, you get results which are significantly out of line with the conventional picture in the newspapers.

British unemployment, as is well known, has come down a long way since the peak in 1993; but it has not fallen as much as the government figures would suggest. German unemployment, by contrast, as is equally well known, has been rising irresistibly since 1991, and stands at an alarmingly high historic level; but it is not as high as government figures say.

Thus, in 1995, British unemployment was 8.1 per cent by the national definition, but 8.7 per cent by the international definition. German unemployment in that year was 9.4 per cent by the national definition, but only 8.2 per cent by the international definition.

In other words, by internationally recognised criteria, unemployment was at that time larger in Britain than in Germany. And, of course, unemployment was much larger in Britain than in West Germany, given that the all-German figures are massively skewed by the collapse of employment in East Germany.

In 1996, the national figure for German unemployment was 10.3 per cent, whereas the national figure for British unemployment was 7.4 per cent; but according to the standardised definition, German unemployment was 9.1 per cent in the autumn of 1996, and British unemployment was 7.9 per cent.

This does not, of course, alter what is politically the most important fact, that unemployment has fallen and is falling in Britain, whereas it remains painfully high in Germany. But it is likely that the real discrepancy between British and German unemployment today is still substantially less than would be suggested by the national figures or by government propaganda.

The TUC viewpoint

Britain's trades union federation, the Trades Union Congress, goes much further and argues, in a study of the UK's jobs record, that the real level of effective unemployment in Britain is much higher than is implied by the unemployment figures. It claims that the true measure should include, not just the number of people who are registered unemployed, but also those who would like a job but have given up trying to find one. By this standard, effective unemployment in Britain is roughly twice the official figure and much higher than in either Germany or France.

The quarterly Labour Force Survey, which gives an estimate of unemployment according to the standardised ILO/OECD definition ('U1'), also gives an estimate of the larger total, including both the officially unemployed and those who are not registered but would like a job ('U3'). By this broader measure, there were 2.23m officially unemployed in Britain in the autumn of 1996, but another 2.25m who would like to work, giving a 'U3' figure of 4.47m, or 14.7 per cent.

In most other European countries, the numbers of people who would like a job but have given up looking is much smaller. In Germany in 1995 it was 850,000, and in France only 340,000.

Table Six: Wanting Work in Britain 1993-96

	ILO Unemployed	Inactive, Want Work	Total
Autumn 1993	2842	2066	4908
Autumn 1996	2226	2247	4473
Change 1993-96	- 22%	+ 9%	- 9%

Table Seven: Why People who Want a Job are Inactive

	Autumn 1993	Autumn 1996	Change
Discouraged	185	138	- 25%
Long-term sick/disabled	499	702	+ 41%
Family/home	750	735	- 2%
Students	212	235	+ 11%
Other	420	436	+ 6%
Total	2066	2247	+ 9%

Table Eight: International Comparisons 1993-95
'U3' measures of all who want to work

	UK	France	Germany
1993	16.1%	12.5%	8.7%
1994	16.0%	13.9%	9.9%
1995	15.1%	13.1%	10.1%

Sources: TUC and Labour Force Surveys 1993-95

There are many reasons why people may have given up looking for work; but one of the largest categories in the autumn of 1996 was that of the long-term sick or disabled, which stood at 702,000, an increase of 203,000 or 41 per cent since the autumn of 1993. The TUC argues that this very steep increase is a reflection of the government's increasingly intense efforts to tighten the criteria for the official unemployment count. But in any case, the corollary of the large U3 figure is that it shows up a fall in the labour participation rate almost unmatched in Europe.

Moreover, the total number of jobs (including the self-employed) has fallen in Britain by 4.8 per cent since 1990 (before the recession), whereas in France the total number of jobs is down only 0.6 per cent, despite its much higher unemployment.

So though there has been a fall in unemployment, the economic recovery in Britain has not been accompanied by a corresponding rise in employment, and the National Institute for Economic and Social Research (NIESR) has conceded that in terms of job creation 'the UK does not appear to perform particularly well'.

'Government claims on jobs', said the TUC study, 'ignore the huge loss of jobs in the UK in the recession of the early 1990s, far greater than most other economies in the rest of the EU.

'Even today there are significantly fewer people in work in the UK than before the recession'.

The European Commission study

Whatever the shortcomings of the official unemployment figures, there is no doubt that unemployment in Britain has come down. The question is, why has it come down? Has there been some structural change in the functioning of the UK labour market? And what is the outlook for the future?

These are some of the questions tackled in the recent study of the UK labour market by Mr Peter Robinson of the London School of Economics. It is one of the first of a series of detailed reports on labour markets in all the EU countries, published by the European Commission. Together they represent a follow-up to the 1993 Delors White Paper on *Growth, Competitiveness, Employment*, when rising mass unemployment was first starting to cause alarm in Europe, and to the job-promotion prescriptions of the 1994 Essen Summit.

The starting point of the LSE study is the wide-ranging series of labour market reforms enacted by the Conservative government which came to power in 1979. The most important of these reforms were aimed at curbing the rights and powers of trades unions: restrictions on the types of industrial action including secondary picketing; the abolition of the closed shop; compulsory democracy for union members; the abolition of minimum wages and the Wages Councils; and some reduction of protection against unfair dismissal.

Inevitably, one of the central questions in the LSE study is this: what have been the repercussions of these labour market reforms, and in particular, how far has the fall in Britain's unemployment been linked to them?

The LSE study suggests in its conclusions that the decline in unemployment in Britain has been due to a combination of two factors: the success of some supply-side reforms, and a macro-economic policy which has been supportive of economic growth and an expansion of employment.

And it goes on to make the optimistic prediction that unemployment in Britain could continue to decline and might, by the year 2000, fall to around 5-6 per cent. If so, this would be roughly half the unemployment rate in 1993, and would mean that Britain would be meeting the target set by the Commission in its 1993 White Paper, when it called for a halving of unemployment by the year 2000.

The downside of the decline in unemployment is that it has been accompanied by a widening of income inequalities, which the study describes as 'one of the main unresolved issues in the UK'.

A detailed reading of the report suggests, however, that its real conclusions are a good deal more qualified than the above summary would suggest.

It says that the prediction, that British unemployment could perhaps fall to 5-6 per cent by the year 2000, is 'a reasonably optimistic assessment'. But elsewhere it raises questions which would cast doubt on such an upbeat outlook.

It makes clear that there is no evidence, or at least no consensus among economists, that there has been any shift in the underlying or 'natural' rate of unemployment in Britain, and no shift in the existing trade-off between unemployment and inflation.

In which case, it may be difficult to argue that there has been any radical step-change in the efficient functioning of the British economy.

In fact, there is no consensus between economists on what the natural rate of unemployment is now, let alone whether it has changed.

The estimates of the British experts currently range from 3.5 per cent to 7-8 per cent. If the true figure is in the top half of that range, it will be difficult for unemployment to fall to 5-6 per cent.

The OECD, by contrast, in its *Lessons from Member Countries' Experience* discussed in a previous section, was confident that the structural rate of unemployment had come down in Britain, as well as in Ireland, in the Netherlands and in New Zealand. On the other hand, it still put the structural rate of unemployment in Britain at 7 per cent in 1996.

The OECD defines structural unemployment as the lowest level that unemployment can fall to, without triggering an acceleration in wage inflation.

Moreover, the LSE study questions how far the decline in unemployment so far can be attributable to the government's labour market reforms, or whether it may not be mainly due to other factors. Perhaps, for example, there has been a shift in the international context, related to the recessions of the early 1980s and the early 1990s, inducing parallel changes in Britain and other countries. Perhaps it is connected to the sharp decline in union membership in Britain, which has dropped from nearly 60 per cent of all employees in 1979 to 38 per cent in 1994. Or perhaps, above all and most crucially, it is related to a reasonable pace of economic recovery from recession.

Productivity

The good news is that there has been a sharp decline in strike activity in Britain since the 1980s. But while the timing of the decline in strike activity may suggest a direct connection with the government's reforms of labour market law, the LSE study points out that a similar decline in strikes occurred in most industrial countries without labour market reforms, and it suggests that the main causal explanation may be the presence throughout the industrialised world of low inflation and high unemployment. 'The UK's new legislative framework may play an additional role', it adds kindly.

At the same time, there has been a substantial improvement in the growth of productivity in the UK, not only in relation to the past, but also in relation to other industrialised countries. In manufacturing, UK productivity grew by 4 per cent a year in the 1980s and early 1990s, (up from only 1 per cent a year in 1973-79), compared with an average of 2.8 per cent in 11 other countries. 'The evidence for a trend improvement in the UK's productivity performance has become more compelling over time', it says.

But the LSE study questions how far this improvement can be linked to the labour market reforms. 'It is the recession of the early 1980s which provided the shock to management and lowered the ability of labour to resist attempts to eliminate over-manning and restrictive practices across all companies, unionised and non-unionised. Increased product market competition has played an important supporting role in maintaining the pressure for improvement; and so perhaps has the [labour market] legislation.

> 'To the extent that the industrial relations legislation has made a contribution to the relative improvement in productivity growth rates in the British economy, this suggests an uncomfortable trade-off, in that the decline in the coverage of collective bargaining and in union density has also contributed to the increase in wage inequality.
>
> 'If the shock of the early 1980s recession was the primary driving force behind the productivity improvements, this suggests an even more troubling trade-off, as that recession heralded the arrival of mass unemployment with all the associated social costs.
>
> 'The 'productivity miracle' was bought at a high price and a legitimate question is to ask is whether more could have been done to assist and compensate the losers'.

Inflation

Similarly, the study is sceptical whether the government's labour market reforms have made it any easier to combat wage inflation. It says that the subdued rate of wage inflation during the recent recovery has led to a degree of optimism that the trade-off between unemployment and inflation might have improved. And yet the facts do not yet support that supposition. It required an increase of two percentage points in unemployment to shave four percentage points off the rate of increase in average earnings between 1981 and 1983; and it again required an increase of two percentage points in unemployment to shave four percentage points of the rate of increase in average earnings between 1991 and 1993.

'There was no sign', says the report, 'that any increase in labour market 'flexibility' had made the process of reducing inflation any less costly in the early 1990s when compared with the early 1980s'.

Inequality

After 1979 a 'dramatic' dispersion in wages opened up, which was out of line with historical experience and with the experience of other European countries, though not the United States. This may be partly due to a shift in the balance of supply and demand against unskilled manual workers, though it is difficult to track this factor, since the changes in the wage premium attaching to higher qualifications appear to explain only a small part of the increase in inequality since 1979.

There is little doubt, however, that institutional changes have also played a role. The decline in unionisation may account for about one fifth of the increase in wage inequality in the 1980s; and other changes in labour market institutions, such as a reduction in minimum wage rates and the eventual abolition of most minimum wage protection in 1993, the abandonment of incomes policies for the private sector after 1979, and the increased decentralisation of pay bargaining, will all have played a role, says the study.

> 'However, in practice in the UK little of the increase in wage inequality is explained by increased returns to qualifications. Internationally there appears to be little solid evidence that countries where earnings inequality is lower have lower levels of employment or higher levels of unemployment for more vulnerable groups in the labour market.
>
> 'It is not obvious, therefore, that the increase in wage inequality has enabled the UK to 'buy' higher levels of employment or lower levels of unemployment'.

8. The Success of The Netherlands

The Netherlands is obviously a classic example of the so-called Rhineland Model. It is a strongly consensual society, and it gives an important negotiating and consultative role to such quasi-corporatist institutions as the trades unions and the employers' federation. It is strongly committed to notions of social solidarity, and it expresses these notions through high and progressive taxation, large transfers, and a costly welfare state.

And yet the Netherlands, like the UK and Ireland, is one of the economic success stories in Europe today, and a notable exception to the general picture of gloom. While many European Union countries seem to be stuck in a kind of unemployment trap, unemployment in the Netherlands has remained modest throughout the recent turn-down, and it is now falling again; its economic growth has recovered, and is already rising again.

The fundamental reason why the Dutch are doing better than many of their neighbours, is that they started to grapple in an intelligent (and consensual) way with their economic problems 15 years ago; not in response to the recent recession, but in response to the previous recession of the early 1980s.

Like other countries, the Netherlands went through a period of stagflation in the 1970s, brought on by the oil shocks, and made worse by short-term expansionary policies. Moreover, in the wake of the boom of

Table Nine: Economic & Employment Growth (%)

	1981-85	1986-90	1991-95	1996-98
GDP Growth				
Netherlands	1.3	3.2	2.2	3.0
EU 15	1.5	3.3	1.5	2.2
USA	3.0	2.9	1.9	2.7
Jobs Growth				
Netherlands	- 0.5	2.2	1.4	2.0
EU 15	- 0.3	1.4	- 0.6	0.4
USA	1.5	2.1	1.0	1.6

Source: OECD, *Economic Outlook*, June 1997

the 1950s and 1960s, the Dutch had created a social security system which was elaborate, generous and expensive.

Wassenaar

When the economy turned down in the early 1980s, therefore, the budget deficit and unemployment both soared out of control. So in a classic consensual response to crisis, the government, the employers and the trade unions came together with the 1982 Wassenaar agreement, which laid the foundations for a long period of wage restraint, tax cutting, and control of social security benefits. In addition the government put new efforts into deregulating the economy, increasing its flexibility and introducing more competition.

At the same time (1982) the government established the link between the Dutch Guilder and the Deutsche Mark; a move which has kept inflation and interest rates low, and helped attract a large flow of investment from abroad. Indeed, the Netherlands has virtually had a *de facto* monetary union with Germany for the past 15 years, and have benefited enormously from it.

As a result of the combined effects of internal reform and external stability, the Netherlands has outperformed most of the rest of the EU, in terms of GDP growth since 1991, and in terms of job creation since the mid-1980s. What is more, it has also outperformed the United States, in both GDP growth and job creation, since the mid-1980s. Unemployment in the Netherlands rose by 1.2 per cent between 1991 and 1996, whereas it went up by 3.6 per cent in Germany and 3 per cent in France. This was in part a reflection of the fact that real wages declined by 0.6 per cent in the Netherlands, but went up by 8.0 per cent in Germany and 3.7 per cent in France.

The burden of government spending on the rest of the economy has been cut back from 57.6 per cent of GDP in 1981 to 49.4 per cent in 1997; while the budget deficit has been cut back from 5.4 per cent of GDP to 2.3 per cent over the same period. In both cases the Netherlands started out in a worse state than the EU average, and ended up in a better state.

For while government spending has been declining in the Netherlands since the early 1980s, it has been rising since that point in France, and since 1990 very steeply in Germany: the declining Dutch spending curve crossed the rising French line in 1995, and the German in 1996.

The main objective of tax policy has been to reduce non-wage labour costs, especially for workers at the bottom end of the market. Thus employers' social security contributions have been brought down from 20 per cent of wages in 1989 to 7.9 per cent in 1994, whereas employees' contributions have been increased from 21 per cent to 31.9 per cent in the same period.

General Government Expenditure (in % of GDP)

Source: Goldman Sachs

And yet spending cuts have been achieved in the Netherlands without sacrificing the principle of redistribution of incomes. The entry rate of income tax was cut in 1994 from 14 per cent to 7 per cent (well below the entry rate in Germany — 27.8 per cent), but the top rate has stayed at 60 per cent (above the top rate in Germany — 57 per cent, and far above the top rate in Britain — 40 per cent).

The improvements in the economic performance of the Netherlands have been brought about by cutting profits taxes as well as taxes on labour, and by cutting back the value of social security payments for unemployment, for disability benefits, and for sickness pay. In addition the government has strengthened the cartel laws, opened up competition in various sectors through deregulation, liberalisation and privatisation (for example, in telecoms), extended shop opening hours, and reduced and simplified various laws and regulations.

The knock-on effects of wage restraint, tax cuts and greater flexibility, have included:

- a significant recovery of profitability
- a strong recovery of the investment ratio
- strong growth of new businesses
- a strong increase in international competitiveness
- and confidence on the part of consumers and producers.

'Thus', in the words of a recent article by the Confederation of Netherlands Industry and Employers, 'an increasingly flexible and dynamic economy was created. This does not mean that all the changes were uncontested. Many demonstrations have been held but, through the years, the majority of the Dutch population has been convinced of the need for these changes and has supported them'.

It is not surprising, therefore, that the Netherlands is one of the four countries singled out for praise by the OECD in its recent *Lessons from Member Countries' Experience,* discussed in section 5.

So any free-market analyst who questions the viability of the Rhineland Model, needs to do two things:

- first, deal with the fact that the current success of the Netherlands has been achieved, not in spite of, but by engaging to maximum advantage the essentially political and co-operative characteristics of the Rhineland system;
- and second, explain why other Rhineland-Model countries could not do as well.

Goldman Sachs

The American bank Goldman Sachs has addressed both these questions, in a recent analysis by its European Economics department entitled 'The New Dutch Model — a Blueprint for Continental Europe?'

They start with the presumption that the consensus-based system characteristic of the continental model 'has come to be seen as inferior to the more competitive and de-centralised system of the Anglo-Saxon countries'; they then concede that 'the Dutch economy has done surprisingly well'; but their verdict on the prospects for the Rhineland Model in other continental countries is nevertheless essentially pessimistic.

'We conclude', they say, 'that other continental European countries are unlikely to exhibit a capacity and determination for reforms similar to that of the Netherlands. In our view, it is more likely that procrastination will eventually render the existing structures in these countries unsustainable and induce market forces finally to sweep them away. This will leave countries with a more de-centralised system of economic organisation along the lines of the Anglo-Saxon countries, rather than with a streamlined system based on consensus and co-operation'.

They also go on to argue that disparities in the economic performance of different European countries is likely to create problems for the European project for Economic and Monetary Union. They believe that those countries which have adjusted more successfully to the challenges of globalisation, like the Netherlands, will grow faster than those which have failed to adjust. 'Since weaker countries will lobby strongly for an easy monetary policy, which stronger countries will find hard to resist, inflation in the Euro zone may be higher than in the old D-Mark zone'.

The Goldman Sachs economists underline that the Netherlands has been 'an interesting exception' to the general European picture of low growth, rising unemployment, and deteriorating public finances. They even concede, admiringly, that overall fiscal consolidation in the Netherlands has been 'even more impressive than in the US', whereas in both Germany and France, by contrast, government deficits have risen during this period.

Moreover, the Dutch current account surplus increased, whereas the United States current account deficit widened dramatically.

Wages and Employment

If there is one key difference between the Rhineland and the Anglo-Saxon models which is more fundamental than all the others, it is in the system of setting wages. This is how the contrast is described by the Goldman Sachs economists.

> 'The competitive model of labour relations existing in the Anglo-Saxon countries combines a high degree of flexibility in hiring and firing with wage bargaining at the firm level, relatively high managerial autonomy, and financial incentives such as bonuses to bind workers to their employer. This model gives superior results in a rapidly changing, competitive and heterogeneous environment as it fosters the diffusion of knowledge among firms through frequent job changes.
>
> 'Against this, the co-operative model is characterised by a high degree of employment protection, centralised wage bargaining, co-determination in firms, and strong income protection. This model has advantages in an environment with stable economic conditions and homogeneous preferences of workers and employers, where the accumulation of firm-specific knowledge through low job turnover is more important.

'In recent years, the more flexible Anglo-Saxon model', say the men from Goldman Sachs, 'has been able to adjust better to increased international competition than the rigid German model'.

The Netherlands, it appears, is an exception to this rule. For the master key to the achievement of the Dutch, in turning round the economy and the public finances, has been their success in mobilising all the positive aspects of the Rhineland Model to secure, over a period of years, nationally-negotiated agreements on wage restraint. A characteristic example of this was 1993, when the 'social partners' (the government, the trade unions, and the employers) agreed that there would be little room for wage increases in the following year.

Formally, wage negotiations in the Netherlands take place at sector level. But in addition there is organised co-ordination between unions and employers at national level to reach a consensus on 'sensible' wage growth, and these guidelines are then fed into the detailed wage negotiations lower down.

It is this centralised co-ordination, according to Goldman Sachs, which is one of the keys to the Dutch success in keeping wages under control. For they argue that the optimum in wage-setting is either a completely de-centralised system (as in America), where competition between firms and workers pushes wages to a market-clearing level; or else a highly centralised system, where wages can be kept under negotiated control.

They claim that Germany has the worst of all worlds, because wage bargaining there takes place at a semi-centralised level, by industry or region, and the government and central bank are supposed not to interfere in the process.

Goldman Sachs also cite two other important features of the labour scene in the Netherlands. On the one hand, far more workers are part-timers in the Netherlands than in the rest of Europe; the proportion used to be 15 per cent in 1975 and 25 per cent in the mid-1980s, and it is now about 35 per cent. At the same time, there has been a large increase in temporary workers, who are hired through the proliferating temporary work agencies. Goldman Sachs argues that these are positive factors, which make important contributions in ensuring labour flexibility and wage stabilisation in the Netherlands.

The OECD, however, is not sure whether such a high proportion of part-time work is a virtue, or a symptom of an economic or social problem. What it is sure about, is that the normal definitions of unemployment are quite inadequate to capture the full extent of the problems of the Dutch labour market scene. For while there has been a decline in officially-defined unemployment, this has been offset by increases in the numbers of people receiving disability benefit or enrolled in early retirement schemes.

The disability scheme seems to have been used by both employers and employees as a disguised alternative to unemployment. And although the government has moved to restrict access to the disability scheme, and to reduce the level of the benefits, the 'disabled' still represent well over 10 per cent of the broad work force.

What this means is that 'broad unemployment' in the Netherlands, that is, all the unemployed, plus the inactive receiving a social security benefit, plus those enrolled in job creation programmes; all these together have amounted to over 25 per cent of the broad labour force for a decade.

In the last analysis, Goldman Sachs argues, a flexible and efficient version of the Rhineland Model is only possible in a small and relatively homogeneous country.

> 'Thus, the smaller the country and the more equal the income distribution, the greater the chance for consensus and co-operation to support adjustment to a changing economic environment. In Germany, where the recent successful performance of the Dutch economy has attracted some attention, society has become more heterogeneous, and the income distribution more unequal since unification.

'Hence the co-operative model, which may have performed still satisfactorily in the former West Germany, has been seriously malfunctioning in united Germany. At present there is no indication that Germany would reach a social consensus about adjustments to fiscal, labour, and social policies as far-reaching as undertaken in the Netherlands in the course of the last 15 years.

'In our view, Germany will have no other choice but to move towards the more de-centralised and competitive Anglo-Saxon model suitable for larger economies. This implies further de-centralisation of the wage formation process; and across-the-board reduction of social benefits with less emphasis on the fine-tuning of instruments; and a cut in top income and corporate tax rates rather than specific tax relief designed to improve employment'.

We shall return to this sweeping judgment by the Goldman Sachs economists in the next chapter, on Germany.

9. The Difficulties of Germany

Germany's current very high level of unemployment is in some sense the central issue in our enquiry. It seems a particularly shocking and surprising reversal, because we are accustomed to think of Germany as a country of low unemployment. And just because Germany has been for so long the most powerful and most successful economy in Europe, the visitation of high unemployment seems to pose, in the starkest terms, the question at the heart of the debate about the viability of the Rhineland Model.

And yet, of course, the traditional picture of Germany as a country of low unemployment is not entirely accurate. Yes, there was a period when Germany had virtually full employment, with an unemployment rate of 1 per cent or less; but that was over 20 years ago, in the 1960s and early 1970s. Since the mid-1970s, however, unemployment in Germany has been an increasingly difficult problem, because the underlying rate of unemployment has surged up in three distinct phases, and each phase has appeared to establish a new, higher plateau.

The first surge came in 1975, after the first oil shock, when the unemployment rate moved up to 4.7 per cent, or 1.1m people. The rate then declined to 3.8 per cent in 1980; but it rose steeply once more in 1985 after the second oil shock to 9.3 per cent or 2.3m people. Again, unemployment slowly declined, but only to 7.2 per cent. The third surge began in 1990 after German unification, and rose by 1996 to 11.5 per cent or 4m people.

Of course, a substantial part of this most recent surge can be directly attributed to the collapse of employment in the former East Germany, which brought with it over 1m registered jobless. But in the years since unification, there has been some convergence between the unemployment rates in East and West, while unemployment in West Germany has grown during the recent recession from 6.3 per cent or 1.7m people in 1991, to 10.1 per cent or 2.8m in 1996.

Free-market critics of the Rhineland model claim that this trend demonstrates the need for wholesale deregulation in Germany. But the IFO Economic Research Institute, which has carried out a study of the German labour market for the European Commission, maintains that neither the problem nor the solution is as simple as that. It argues that a reduction in non-wage labour costs, notably by cutting social insurance contributions, would increase employment. But it points out that there is no consensus in Germany on the causes of unemployment, nor on its cure.

Unemployment in Germany 1960-96 (in thousands)

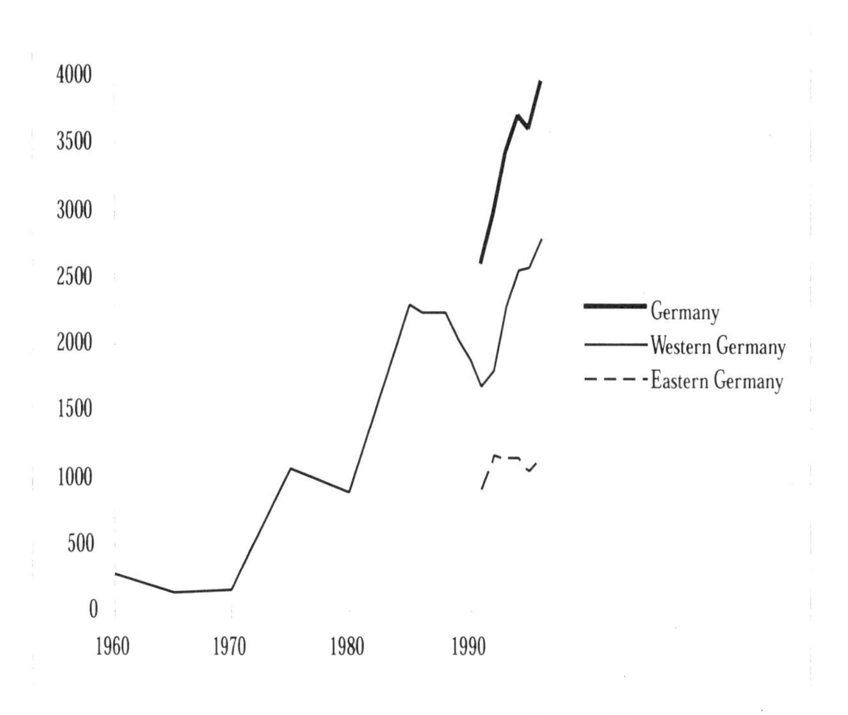

Source: European Commission

The IFO study examines four possible causes:

1. Too little flexibility in the labour market;

2. Supply-side shocks, like adverse movements in oil prices or the exchange rate;

3. Labour supply shocks, like net immigration; or

4. Hysteresis — the unemployed become inherently less employable.

But the IFO economists conclude that none of these causes is enough by itself to explain the phenomenon, even if each of them played a contributory role.

What emerges clearly from the study, however, is the perception that the political debate in Germany has taken on a new urgency. In the past, it says, there was a widespread assumption that unemployment would be taken care of by a combination of faster economic growth and dynamic innovation on the part of German industrial companies. This was, of course, the line of least resistance: with rising prosperity, public opinion was more prepared to accept the budgetary costs, in taxation and social security contributions, of paying unemployment benefit or early retirement, than to make significant reforms in wage policy or social policy.

But there is a new mood in Germany today, says the study, and one reason is the growing awareness that demographic shifts will cause increasingly serious social and budgetary problems in future. Not only is the German population expected to decline during the next half century, perhaps by 11m people by 2040, but it is also ageing, so that the proportion of the population over 60 years old is forecast to rise from 20 per cent now to 30 per cent by the year 2020.

Therefore, the financing of pensions will be an increasingly serious problem. Early retirement used to be promoted as a soft option for disguising or even reducing unemployment. But now the cost of retirement is perceived as a serious problem in its own right, so that even if early retirement appears to alleviate the unemployment problem, it makes the retirement problem worse.

The new mood perceived by the IFO team derives from the widely accepted conviction that 'a reduction in unemployment will require great efforts from all political forces'. This does not mean that there is yet any agreement, either on the causes of unemployment, or on the right policies for reducing it. 'Nevertheless', says the study, 'the promotion of new jobs seems to be more important than the creation of social equity'.

Of course, if that really is the unavoidable trade-off, between jobs and equity, then it implies that there may be a conflict between the social virtues of the Rhineland model and the economic virtues of the market.

One social initiative which was launched for promoting employment was the *Alliance for Jobs* proposed by the IG Metall trade union. The idea was a three-way agreement between workers, employers and the government, which offered to swap wage moderation for job creation. Companies would promise to create 300,000 new jobs, to hire 30,000 long-term unemployed, to increase the number of traineeships by 5 per cent each year, and not to lay off workers in the next three years. The government would undertake not to reduce unemployment benefit. And in return, IG Metall promised to agree wage increases in 1997 below the rate of inflation.

It seems this plan has not got off the ground, partly perhaps because the union's proposals looked one-sided and disingenuous. In the first place, the employers federations would be unable to give any binding guarantees on employment; only individual companies could do that. Secondly, the demand that the government should leave the social security system unchanged simply evades the possibility that such reforms may be essential for job creation. Nevertheless, the union has this year made a new proposal, to fight unemployment by cutting the working week.

Goldman Sachs

Foreign free market critics say that Germany's current economic travails, and the reluctance of the political system to grasp the solutions, are a graphic demonstration of what is wrong with the system. Germany is struggling with budgetary problems, they say, mainly because it has a welfare state which is already far too generous, feather-bedding and extravagant, and which will become even more expensive as the German population ages. Germany has high unemployment, they say, because the economy is too regulated, too corporatist, too cosy, too protectionist, and too sclerotic to adapt to the new world of global competition.

As we saw in the section on the Netherlands, the conclusion of the Goldman Sachs economists is crisp, stern and categoric: the German economy may have worked well enough in the past, but now it is incapable of being reformed and adapted for the new circumstances of international competition. Therefore the German model of regulation, welfare and high taxation will simply have to be swept away.

There are three main difficulties with this sweeping judgment:

- it fails to explain why the German model worked so well for so many years, until the massive shock of unification;

- it takes no account of the fact that Germany remains the exporting power-house of Western Europe, which suggests that German industry has somehow managed to remain internationally competitive; and

- it does not explain why the Germans, who were obviously able to adapt to changing circumstances in the past, should be unable to adapt to changing circumstances now.

In short, the verdict and the sentence of the Goldman Sachs economists seem summary, even rash. Time without number, Anglo-Saxon economists have predicted the downfall of the German model, and Germany has repeatedly proved them wrong. During the last half-century, Germany has so long and so consistently been demonstrably one of the world's most successful economies, that an unqualified condemnation needs more than mere assertion.

It is obvious that there are at least three factors at work in Germany's current economic troubles: the recession, from which Germany is now slowly emerging; the many costs of the unification of Germany; and the budgetary constraints in the run-up to Economic and Monetary Union in Europe. The question at stake for our enquiry is whether, or to what extent, these difficulties have been made worse by the characteristics of the 'Rhineland Model'.

The question matters not just for Germany but also for Europe.

First, Germany is by a substantial margin the largest, most powerful, and (until now) most successful economy in the European Union. If the German economy now faces painful and long-lasting difficulties of structural adaptation, this will have enormous economic repercussions for all the other member states of the Union.

Moreover, the medium-term future of the European Union will be largely determined by the success or failure of the project for Economic and Monetary Union. And EMU in turn will depend critically on the ability of all the participating countries, but especially Germany, to adapt to new global conditions and new collective constraints.

Second, it is hard to understate the political implications of the Goldman Sachs verdict. Germany's welfare state can trace its ancestry to the pioneering policies of Bismarck of the 19th Century; and there is no getting round the fact that today's 'Rhineland Model' is the result of a process of sustained and deliberate political choice by the German people. If the Goldman Sachs economists are right, it means that the ineluctable pressures of economic change will also bring about a fundamental restructuring of the political priorities of German society, with potential danger for the social fabric.

Carlin-Soskice

A more complex and subtle diagnosis of Germany's current problems has been published in an article in the National Institute Economic Review, by Wendy Carlin of University College London, and David Soskice of Wissenschaftscentrum für Sozialforschung Berlin.

Their conclusion is that, yes, there is a need for increased flexibility in the German economy, but that, no, radical deregulation by itself is not the answer, for it would threaten features of the system which give German companies a comparative advantage.

'On any reasonable analysis of Germany's 'present discontents', their cause does not lie primarily in micro-economic inflexibilities', they say, 'but in a combination of aggregate wage determination and macro-economic policy-making'.

The central problem, according to their analysis, is that there are serious short-comings in the institutional mechanisms for managing the German economy. On the one hand, there seems no longer to be an effective system of wage restraint on the part of the trades unions; on the other hand, and in response, the authorities are virtually constrained to pursue deflationary macro-economic policies.

After unification in 1989, the German trades unions rode the accompanying boom to secure large wage increases three years running: 4.8 per cent in 1990, 6.0 per cent in 1991 and 5.8 per cent in 1992. This wage surge was accompanied by a steep decline in company profits, and some commentators have read it as a symptom of a breakdown of the post-war social consensus in Germany.

As the economy then over-heated (real GDP rose 5.7 per cent in 1990 and 5.0 per cent in 1991), the Bundesbank pushed up interest rates and drove the economy into recession. Wage inflation then declined sharply, but the Bundesbank only reduced interest rates very gradually, despite the depth of the recession (in 1993 real GDP fell by 1.1 per cent).

One of the characteristics of the 'Rhineland Model' is that it is supposed to display a high degree of cooperation between the main economic actors, notably the government, employers and trades unions. And though in Germany there is no national system of formal co-ordination in the wage bargaining system between the two sides of industry, or between them and the Bundesbank or the government, in practice the West German system has in the past worked well to provide a high degree of informal economy-wide co-ordination.

So what is striking about the Carlin-Soskice diagnosis of today's situation is that it is couched in the adversarial language of institutional conflict. 'The Bundesbank', they say, 'sought to punish the unions for excessive wage increases, and the government for excessive levels of borrowing'. And the implication of their analysis is that there may be some truth in the claim sometimes made, that independent central banks, whose primary commitment is to monetary stability (like the Bundesbank), may therefore tend to have a bias in favour of deflation.

This is connected to one of the factors inhibiting reflation in Germany today, which is that the Bundesbank and the government are unsure whether the unions are able to deliver wage restraint. And the reason is that in 1990-92 the unions showed that they were unwilling to deliver wage restraint. Moreover, according to Carlin-Soskice, there has over the past 15 years been a power shift away from the unions towards the company-based works councils; these are biased in favour of the skilled workers, whose status gives them more job security than the unskilled, and who are therefore significantly less vulnerable to the threat of deflationary measures by the Bundesbank.

> 'Thus aggregate wage moderation, let alone a reduction in real unit labour costs adequate to restore profitability and maintain employment, is indeed difficult for the unions to deliver'.

Another factor is that the government cannot use fiscal policy to reflate, because it is constrained by the budgetary convergence criteria of the Maastricht conditions for EMU. But in any case West German authorities have never been really comfortable with discretionary reflation. In the past, the German economy has been pulled out of previous deflationary episodes by exogenous locomotives: the Reagan boom of the early 1980s, or the unification expenditures of the early 1990s. But in the mid-1990s, say Carlin-Soskice, it is hard to see where external reflation is going to come from.

Thus far the Carlin-Soskice analysis touches some common ground both with the DIW study discussed in the section on the international context, and with the Goldman Sachs article discussed in the section on the Netherlands. Like DIW, they put heavy emphasis on the importance of macro-economic policy and growth; if so, it remains to be seen what will be the effects as and when growth returns. Like Goldman Sachs, they imply that there has been a breakdown in a key feature of the German system, which is co-operation. If so, it is perhaps largely attributable to the shock of unification; the question which has yet to be answered is whether cooperation can be restored.

East Germany

The unification of Germany is in fact the third major factor that they focus on, and they say it is a massive and still unresolved problem. This is not just because of the vast scale of the budgetary transfers from West to East Germany (some 4.0-4.5 per cent of GDP in the years since unification), but mainly because, despite these transfers, and despite the imposition of West German institutions, East Germany is still failing to transform itself into a West German-type economy based on an internationally-competitive exporting industry.

West Germany is still the exporting power-house of Western Europe, and its industry in some ways encapsulates the characteristics of the 'Rhineland Model': an industrial relations and training system which favours a co-operative and highly-skilled work-force; a corporate governance system which provides companies with long-term finance; and an industrial ethos which encourages technology transfer, inter-company cooperation, and deep relational contracts. But these institutional characteristics are not being adequately replicated in East Germany.

At the time of unification, East German industry seemed well placed to expand through its existing markets in Eastern Europe. And since many big West German companies were planning to invest in East Germany, the government and the employers' associations endorsed the principle of rapid equalisation of Eastern wages on those in the West. But after unification, the industry and the markets of East Germany both collapsed, and West German companies shelved their investment plans.

Productivity in East Germany has improved since unification, from 20 per cent of the West German level in 1991 to 53 per cent in 1995; but though unit labour costs in manufacturing came down to 30 per cent above the Western level in 1993, there has been no improvement since then. Unless enough Western companies invest in the East, Eastern industry will not be able to acquire the characteristics typical of West German industry. The dilemma is that wage rates in Poland and the Czech Republic are not merely below official wage rates in East Germany, they are also below the level of unemployment benefit and social assistance in East Germany.

The final judgment of Carlin-Soskice on the unification experiment is pessimistic. They do not quite say that it has failed; but they do say: 'There is no easy way out'.

The fourth source of anxiety on the West German scene, according to Carlin-Soskice, is over the future of the less skilled workers. Industrial job losses in the recent recession were concentrated on the less skilled workers, and companies are engaged where feasible on relocating less skilled activities to low-wage countries of Eastern Europe. As a result, unemployment is now significantly higher among the unskilled than among the general work force.

The problem of the unskilled

This question of the problem of the employment of unskilled workers has been independently illuminated by a research paper by Professor Stephen Nickell.

He found that unemployment rates for the unskilled were broadly similar over time in Germany and the US, though rather higher in Britain. But among employed workers, the earnings of the unskilled rose substantially in Germany during the 1980s, whereas they fell substantially in the US. As a result, the earnings of German workers in the bottom 10 per cent are, in terms of purchasing power parity, around twice the earnings of American workers in the bottom 10 per cent. In other words, the working poor have been getting richer in Germany, but poorer in the US.

At the same time, the spread of earnings between the skilled and the unskilled, which increased substantially in Britain and the US, remained much more compressed in Germany.

Table Ten: International Test Scores (%)

Distribution of scores in international mathematics tests of 13 year olds, 1963-64

Score out of 70	USA	Germany	England
< 5	22	8	24
6 - 30	62	59	49
31 - 51	14	30	22
< 51	1	3	5
Mean	16	25	19

Scores in international mathematics tests of 13 year olds, 1990

	USA	Switzerland	England
Average	59.5	70.8	55.3
Top decile	89.3	93.3	82.7
Bottom decile	32	50.7	29.3

Literacy levels of employees, 1995 (Level 1 is illiterate)

Literacy level	USA	Germany
4/5	22.7	22.4
3	33.9	41.6
2	25.6	30.7
1	17.8	5.3

Source: Nickell, *Policy Studies* No. 1, 1996

On the face of it, this is a puzzling situation. For it is not obvious why the general trend of a relative shift against unskilled workers has not shown up in wage inequality in Germany, nor why German employers, who are just as exposed to international competition as their American competitors, should be willing to pay twice as much for unskilled workers.

The deduction drawn by Professor Nickell is that, if unskilled German workers are paid more, it cannot be because German employers are indifferent to their labour costs; therefore it must be because unskilled workers in Germany are worth more; and he cites research which indicates that unskilled German workers may be significantly more productive than their Anglo-Saxon counterparts.

If so, the first and most obvious reason is that they are better educated up to a certain level. For while at the top end of the achievement ladder educational results in Germany are no better than those in Britain or America, at the bottom end they are much better. In international maths tests, German 13-year-old pupils have done measurably better than Britons or Americans on average; but far fewer of them scored very low marks. Similarly, illiteracy is far less common among workers in Germany than in the US.

In other words, unskilled workers in Germany are not as unskilled as those in Britain or America.

'The overall conclusion to be drawn', says Professor Nickell, 'from the German experience of the decline in demand for the unskilled, compared to the experiences of the UK and the US, is straightforward. A strong emphasis in the schooling system on sustaining a high level of performance on the part of the bottom half of the ability range, plus a comprehensive system of vocational training, mitigates many of the adverse consequences of a shift in demand away from the unskilled.

Table Eleven: Unemployment by Age, 1995 (%)

Age	Germany	France	UK
15 - 19	7.6	30.8	17.3
20 - 24	8.8	26.5	14.5
All ages	8.2	11.9	8.7

Source: European Commission, Labour Market Studies

'Furthermore, the evidence suggests that the training system requires the schooling system in order to be successful. This suggests that moving their education system in the German direction would certainly help with the low-skill, low-pay problem in both Britain and the US'.

A more general conclusion, of course, could be that deregulation is not the only, nor even necessarily the best, response to the economic and social problems caused by internationalisation and structural change.

Long-term and short-term

One reason why German national figures for unemployment are higher than they would be under the ILO definition, is that some of the unemployed in Germany are not really looking for work, but are in fact waiting for early retirement.

This is a feature of the employment/unemployment scene which distinguishes Germany from most other countries. For older workers, the unemployment register can be the passport to early retirement, because if they spend a period of one year or more ostensibly in unemployment, they can then claim an early pension. The quid pro quo, in the negotiations which lead to this process of lay-offs of the elderly, is that companies agree to keep up their training programmes for young workers.

The net result is that there are fewer men still working after the age of 55 in Germany (52 per cent in 1990) than in the US (65 per cent), while elderly males are over-represented in the long-term unemployed.

But the converse of high unemployment for the elderly is that the level of youth unemployment is significantly lower in Germany than it used to be, as a percentage of total unemployment.

Moreover, this youth unemployment, which has become such a serious scourge in other industrialised countries, is in Germany not merely lower, at 5.6 per cent of the under 25's in 1990, than youth unemployment in the US (11.2 per cent) or Britain (10.1 per cent), but is also, more remarkably, close to the general level of adult unemployment in Germany.

Table Twelve: Youth Unemployment (below 25 years) (%)

	As % of total			*% rate*	
	1974-79	1980-89	1990-93	1979	1990
Germany (W)	25.1	25.4	15.0	4.0	5.6
USA	48.6	39.8	32.3	11.8	11.2
UK	35.5	37.6	30.2	10.3	10.1

Source: NIESR 1/97

10. Recommendations

Far-reaching economic and social reforms are urgently required if Europe is to be able to overcome its problem of mass structural unemployment, and meet the challenge of the rapidly changing and increasingly competitive global market.

In many cases reforms will include deregulation, privatisation, and the opening up of protected or vested interests to the forces of greater competition. But every European country has different structural problems, and will need different detailed reforms: there is no simple reach-me-down prescription which can be applied throughout Europe.

As a general principle, reform should be articulated in terms which take due account of the values of social solidarity and political consent which underlie the so-called Rhineland Model. There is no basis for advocating the wholesale scrapping of the so-called Rhineland Model.

On the contrary, the values of social solidarity and political consent will be of great benefit to European countries, if they can be mobilised to help contain the social strains which are liable to accompany the ultra-rapid structural and technological changes taking place in the world economy.

Since the Rhineland Model is built on principles of negotiation and consent, its reform also needs to be built on the same principles: the process of reform of the Rhineland Model will only be successful if it is based on the same social values of the Rhineland Model, that is to say, social solidarity and political consent. But, by definition, the reform process must mean the surrender of specific vested interests which can no longer be justified. Therefore, it will call for exceptional leadership and vision from politicians, businessmen and trades unionists.

The recommendations outlined below are framed in the belief that European countries should and can reform the Rhineland Model, not abandon it.

The recommendations are set out in four parts: European Union, national governments, the social partners, and the forthcoming British tenure of the presidency of the European Council.

The European Union

Reform of the Rhineland Model will be essential for the success of the European Union's two most important economic programmes, the completion of the Single Market, and Economic and Monetary Union. Both should make enormous contributions to Europe's welfare, but only if European countries succeed in opening up their economies to greater competitiveness, flexibility, growth and employment.

The trade liberalisation process of the Single Market can make a major contribution to job creation, as well as to Europe's competitiveness; it is therefore vital that it be vigorously carried to completion. This will involve far-reaching liberalisation of all markets, and not just labour markets; it is calculated that product markets which are still affected by national restrictions account for about half the European Union's GDP.

Deregulation may be especially valuable in those areas, such as public utilities, where competition can bring major benefits and more employment. It is also vital to ensure that the Single Market for goods is complemented by the single market for capital and labour.

It is hard to overstate the far-reaching implications of Economic and Monetary Union. It will reinforce the single market for goods and services, as well as the single market for finance and capital; it will accelerate the process of economic restructuring and consolidation throughout the Union; and it will inevitably create new impetus for closer fiscal and, indirectly, political integration.

By the same token, however, the breadth and the depth of the economic restructuring implied by EMU will constitute an unprecedented political challenge for the people of Europe. If it is to be successful, it will call for an exceptional degree of adaptability on their part; but if it is, initially, less successful, it will impose profound strains on the fabric of European society.

One of the most important questions about EMU, therefore, is whether it will help deliver a faster rate of economic growth in Europe. If it does, it will ease the inevitable strains of the transition to Monetary Union; it will also make a substantial contribution to reducing the unemployment problem. But these benefits will not come about to the optimum extent, except as the result of deliberate policy. It is therefore vital that there should be serious macro-economic co-ordination between the Member States, with the explicit objective of promoting economic growth.

However, it is also clear that the success of Economic and Monetary Union will also depend heavily on the vigour with which the Member States pursue the reform, deregulation and liberalisation of their economies.

What is more, reform and restructuring will also be a pre-condition for carrying through the programme of enlargement to include the ten countries of Eastern Europe. For unless the social partners can successfully adapt to the new constraints of EMU and the global economy, there could be a real danger of a backlash against European integration, with a risk in particular that Eastern enlargement could be in jeopardy.

Most of the necessary reforms will have to be carried out by the Member States. But there will be a need for a complementary role for the European Union, in the co-ordination of budgetary and macro-economic policy, in mutual surveillance and encouragement in the identification of best practice in micro-economic reform, in the development of the European infrastructure, and in the promotion of Europe-wide training and education programmes to promote greater labour mobility.

The member states

European countries will and should maintain their welfare states. But the costs of these welfare states are already, in many cases, excessive. It seems clear that the combined burden of taxation and social security contributions is, in many countries, by now counter-productively high. And if nothing is done, the ageing of the populations in Europe will make these welfare systems even more expensive in future.

Member states will therefore need to examine ways of reducing their overall tax burdens. As a result, they will have to engage in a radical re-think of their welfare arrangements, to decide which of them need to be reformed, which should be slimmed down, and which can be transferred in whole or in part to the private sector.

A greater role must be found for privately-funded pensions, partly because of the escalating costs of unfunded state pensions. Moreover, the creation of private pension funds can also become an important engine for the modernisation of, and investment in, the wealth-creating sectors of the European economies.

The flows of savings into pension funds will be essential for the development of fluid and competitive capital markets, and a vital precondition for the development of venture capital markets.

One type of tax reform which already seems essential, in many countries, will be a reduction of those taxes or social security contributions which increase non-wage labour costs, and which by some calculations could be responsible for as much as one third of current unemployment levels.

Conversely, Member States should avoid any ill-considered competition in tax-cutting, as for example in taxes on corporations or on capital, in the belief that this will enable them to attract more foreign direct investment.

On the contrary, the single most important factor influencing multinational investment is the quality of infrastructure, which in many cases depends heavily on government investment.

In the last resort, European countries, like all industrial countries, will depend for their survival, not on regulation (= protection), nor on welfare (= current transfers), but on the development of human capital (= education and training).

The responsibility for raising levels of general education and basic transferable skills will essentially remain with the state. For while the market can provide education for an élite, and perhaps even for a minority, only the collectivity can provide adequate education for the society as a whole, to meet the needs of the emerging world. In the case of vocational training, by contrast, there must be a bigger role for the private sector, and in particular for the business sector, since future employment will increasingly be knowledge-based.

The social partners

The emerging world of accelerating structural economic change will make huge demands on the cohesion of society. If the Rhineland Model is to play its part in meeting these demands, the social partners will have to play an even larger role, and carry a bigger responsibility, than in the past.

One of the consequences of the speed of economic change is that the centre of gravity of strategic policy-making decisions will unavoidably shift from the exclusive domain of government, towards that of business. In the global economy, national governments have decreasing autonomy to manage their national economies, whereas international business straddles the globe. If European countries are to make a successful adaptation to this world, they will need new forms of partnership between government and business, between local and regional government and business, and between business and the trades unions.

An essential characteristic of these partnerships is that business should acknowledge broader social objectives and responsibilities than the exclusive pursuit of shareholder value. This may come more naturally to businesses with roots in the Rhineland system, than to those in the Anglo-Saxon tradition.

Business will have an essential role, in partnership with government, with local government, and with non-governmental organisations (NGOs), in developing innovative ways to help the long-term unemployed and the least skilled into work.

But since economic growth will in future be increasingly knowledge-based, business will also have a vital role in the realm of education and vocational training, in partnership both with government and with the trades unions. Business will absolutely depend on having access to workers who are highly educated and highly skilled, and should therefore have a larger responsibility for helping design, and in part for providing, the requisite education and training.

Thirdly, government-business partnerships could also have an important part to play in handling the reform of the traditional welfare state. In most European countries, there is a clear need for more privatisation of pension provision, and there may well be more need for private health insurance.

The British presidency

The first six months of 1998, when the British government will be holding the presidency of the European Union, will be marked by two exceptionally important European events: the decision to launch the first wave of the single currency, and the formal opening of membership negotiations with Cyprus and five of the candidate countries from Eastern Europe.

One should not over-estimate what any one member state can achieve during a brief six-month presidency. Nevertheless, the fact that Britain will be in some degree in the limelight at two such key moments, will inevitably focus attention on the ambiguities of the British government's policy towards Europe.

Since Britain will be presiding over these two major turning points, the British government will have an opportunity to re-establish its European credentials in other European capitals, and a duty to re-build public confidence at home in Britain's role in Europe.

In the context of our present enquiry, Britain's credentials in Europe would be strengthened if the government were prepared to recognise not only the need for flexibility but also the legitimacy of the value systems underlying the Rhineland Model, to which most other member states are in various ways committed. There is no point in lecturing the other members of the European Union, whose economic record has generally been far superior to Britain's, that they are mistaken in their political preferences.

It is already clear that Britain will not seek to join the single currency in the first wave. But at that moment when a large majority of the member states will be committing themselves to moving to the final stage of EMU, it will become increasingly implausible for the British government to continue hedging its bets on the project, by hiding behind technical and arbitrary pretexts.

The British government should publicly firm up its political commitment to join the single currency and to do so at the earliest appropriate opportunity. It should also urge on its partners the wider aspects of reform as outlined in this report.

Bibliography

Michel Albert, *Capitalism versus Capitalism*, 1992

Wendy Carlin and David Soskice, 'Shocks to the System: the German Political Economy under Stress' in *National Institute Economic Review*, January 1997

Harry Cowie, Rapporteur, *Private Partnerships and Public Networks in Europe*, Federal Trust Report, 1996

Deutches Institute für Wirtschaftsforschung, *Employment and social policies under international constraints*, A Study for the Ministerie van Sociale Zaken en Werkgelegenheid of the Netherlands, 1996

European Commission, *Growth, Competitiveness, Employment: The Challenges and Ways Forward into the 21st Century*, White Paper, Supplement 6/93 to the EC Bulletin, 1993

European Commission, Annual Economic Report 1997

European Commission, *The Competitiveness of European Industry*, Report from the Directorate-General for Industry, 1997

European Commission, *Labour Market Studies*, Directorate General for Employment, Industrial Relations and Social Affairs, 1997:

- Peter Robinson, *The United Kingdom*
- Ifo Institute for Economic Research, *Germany*

European Round Table of Industrialists, *Benchmarking for Policy-Makers*, 1996

European Round Table of Industrialists, *A Stimulus to Job Creation*, 1997

Goldman Sachs, *The New Dutch Model: A Blueprint for Continental Europe?*, Frankfurt, 1997

McKinsey Global Institute, *Removing Barriers to Growth and Employment in France and Germany*, March 1997

OECD, *Jobs Study*, 1994

OECD, *Employment Outlook*, July 1997

OECD, *Implementing the Jobs Strategy*, 1997:

- *Member Countries' Experience*
- *Lessons from Member Countries' Experience*

S.J. Nickell, 'The Low-Skill, Low-Pay Problem: lessons from Germany for Britain and the US' in *Policy Studies*, Vol. 17, no. 1, 1996

S.J. Nickell, 'Unemployment and Labour Market Rigidities: Europe versus the United States' in *Journal of Economic Perspectives*, 1997

D.J. Snower and G. de la Dehesa (eds), *Unemployment Policy: Government Options for the Labour Market*, CEPR, 1996

Dick Taverne, Rapporteur, *The Pension Time Bomb in Europe*, Federal Trust Report, 1995

TUC, *How well has the UK really performed?*, Occasional Paper, February 1997

Meinhard Wiegel and Stefanie Wahl, *Employment and Unemployment in Germany, Part I: Trends, causes and measures*, Kommission für Zukunftsfragen der Freistaaten Bayern und Sachsen, 1996